WAITANGI

OTHER BOOKS BY PETER SHAW

Art Deco Napier—Styles of the Thirties
Spanish Mission Hastings—Styles of Five Decades
New Zealand Architecture from Polynesian Beginnings to 1990

WAITANGI

PETER SHAW

Photography by Peter Hallett

COSMOS PUBLICATIONS – PO BOX 5153 NAPIER – NZ

First Published in 1992 by

COSMOS PUBLICATIONS
PO Box 5153, NAPIER, NEW ZEALAND

with the assistance of the Waitangi National Trust

National Library of New Zealand
Cataloguing-in-Publication data

Shaw, Peter, 1946-
    Waitangi / Peter Shaw ; photography by Peter Hallett. Napier, N.Z.
Cosmos, 1992
    1 v.
    ISBN 0-908887-07-8 (hbk.)
    ISBN 0-908887-03-5 (pbk.)
    1. Waitangi (N.Z.) --History. 2. Waitangi Treaty House.
3. Dwellings--New Zealand--Northland Region--History.
4. Historic buildings--New Zealand--Northland Region--History.
5. Historic sites--New Zealand--Northland Region--History.
6. Treaty of Waitangi (1840) I. Hallett, Peter, 1922-
II.   Waitangi National Trust (N.Z.) III. Title.
       993.12 (728.8099312)

ISBN 0 908887 07 8 (hard cover)

ISBN 0 908887 03 5 (soft cover)

Foreword

In 1990 New Zealand commemorated the 150th anniversary of the first signings of the Treaty of Waitangi. This significant milestone in our country's history focused attention on the Treaty House at Waitangi, the place where this historic event occurred.

The Treaty House is now a national monument but its chequered history has seen it variously used as a house for the British Resident, Mr James Busby, a family home, a hay shed and a place of both protest and celebration. As part of the 1990 Sesquicentennial celebrations, the Treaty House was restored to a state which now enables the visitor to see it as it was in 1840.

Waitangi is a timely publication for it not only chronicles the history of the house to the present time, but also places it geographically within its magnificent Bay of Islands location. It charts the history of the environs of the house from earliest recorded times. It draws on both Maori oral history and written academic studies. For the first time, it provides an accessible historical survey for the visitor to Waitangi and for the general reader.

As Chairperson of the Waitangi National Trust I welcome this publication which, with its informative maps, plans, reproductions of paintings, historical and modern photographs, brings the history of the Waitangi area and the Treaty House alive.

Dame Catherine Tizard, GCMG, DBE
Governor-General of New Zealand

Dame Catherine Tizard GCMG, DBE
Governor-General of New Zealand

AUTHOR'S NOTE

This book was written to provide an introduction to the Treaty House and its environs. It began as a history of the former British Residency, now known as the Waitangi Treaty House. It soon became apparent that the house, interesting though it is in its own right, could only be properly appreciated within the larger context of the pre-European Maori history of the area and the events which followed the first Maori-European contacts.

As a relatively frequent visitor to Waitangi, I was always frustrated by the lack of readily available historical information about the region. Such material has remained relatively inaccessible to all but professional historians. This book aims to bring it together for the general reader. Hopefully it will encourage New Zealanders to appreciate Waitangi more fully and to introduce overseas visitors to an area of New Zealand which is both visually beautiful and historically fascinating.

The publisher and I wish to acknowledge the assistance of the Waitangi National Trust Board throughout the planning, research, writing and production of this book.

I am grateful to Joan McCracken, Librarian of the Pictorial Reference Service at the Alexander Turnbull Library, Wellington, and to Anne Upton, Assistant Curator of Drawings and Prints at the same institution. Roger Blackley, Curator of Historic New Zealand Art at the Auckland City Art Gallery and Gordon Maitland, Librarian at the Auckland Institute and Museum, both drew my attention to significant illustrative material.

I am particularly indebted to Rodney Hamel for his expert advice and criticism and to Dr Aidan Challis and Dr Anne Salmond for their helpful suggestions. Coral Shaw asked many thought-provoking questions at all stages of the book's gestation. Tim Hallett brought both care and skill to the maps he has contributed. Peter Hallett was, once again, an enthusiastic and thoroughly amenable collaborator, ably assisted by Patrick Sherratt.

Peter Shaw
Auckland
October 1991.

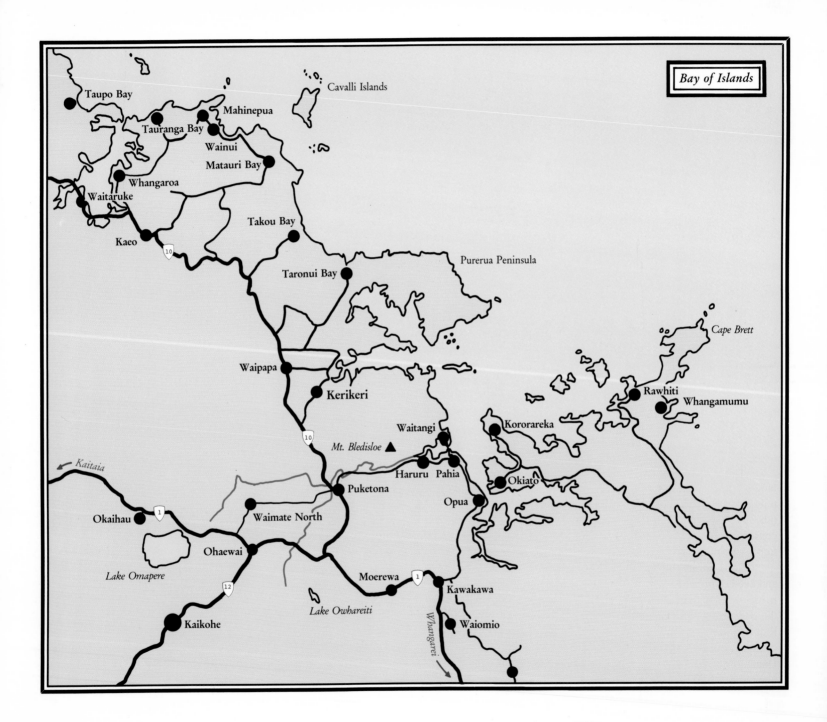

Bay of Islands

Waitangi

The land at Waitangi in the Bay of Islands derives its major significance in New Zealand's history from the signing of the Treaty of Waitangi between representatives of both the British Crown and the **tangata whenua** on February 6th 1840. However it had been inhabited for many years before this and the coast at Waitangi was traditionally valued as a source of food for the various **hapu** who utilised it.

Long before the arrival of European settlers the Ngapuhi tribe gradually achieved dominance of the area around Waitangi. They traced their ancestry from the chief Rahiri whose descendants eventually drove the former inhabitants, the Ngatiawa tribes, from the north thus establishing a Ngapuhi ascendancy. Rahiri, son of Tauramoko, could trace his ancestry back to Nukutawhiti who came to Aotearoa on the canoe Mamari from Hawaiki. It was his wife Hauangiangi who was a daughter of Puhi-kai-ariki, the eponymous ancestor of Ngapuhi.

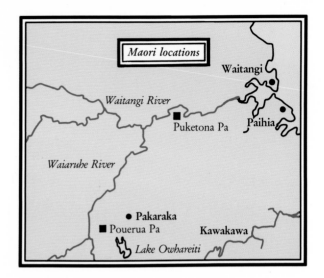

Like many places in New Zealand Waitangi has a long oral record of history in which the traditions of inhabiting tribes are permanently embedded in place names recalling ancestral associations. Earliest recorded specific mention in Maori tradition of Waitangi, which means 'weeping waters', occurs in the story of the birth of Rahiri's son Uenuku. Abandoned as the result of an earlier disobedience, his mother Ahuaiti had only the company of Aniwaniwa, a rainbow, and so when her son was born she gave him the name Uenuku, or rainbow.

Although the child was eventually re-united with his father Rahiri, from whom he learned **karakia**, Uenuku later returned to live at Pouerua Pa with his mother. As an adult he married Kareariki who bore five children, the second of whom was a daughter named Maikuku. Renowned for her beauty she was made tapu and thus could not live among her hapu so was confined to a cave situated on the shoreline at Waitangi. This place, known as Te Ana o Maikuku, was probably situated near the present canoe house at Hobson Bay.

Maikuku was eventually sought out by a man called Hua who, hearing of her fame, determined to find her. This he did by listening to the wailing of **taniwha** which guided him to the very interior of her cave. Maikuku and Hua then moved up from the seashore to a house called Ruarangi. This name means 'two skies' and refers to the meeting of sea and sky at the horizon. Here at Waitangi their first child was born and given the name Te Ra, the Sun, in commemoration of Hua's words to Maikuku, " It is fine, it faces the Sun," which he uttered in an attempt to comfort her having desecrated her formerly tapu dwelling. This land remains memorable today for those very qualities of sunlight and water in relationship to the land reflected in the story of Maikuku.

It was their son Te Ra who was to become the founder of the Ngapuhi hapu called Ngati Rahiri which controlled the inland pa at Pouerua as well as the coastal land at Waitangi and gradually infiltrated all the ancient Ngatiawa territory in the north. The original inhabitants migrated south and today their descendants live in Taranaki as Atiawa and in the Bay of Plenty as Ngatiawa.

It was during the years 1790 to 1820 that the land between Pouerua Pa and Waitangi, connected by the Waitangi River, gradually came under the control of the Ngati Rahiri hapu of Ngapuhi. This was finally achieved when a chief called Ruatara, married Miki, the daughter of Waraki, a Ngatipou chief who lived at Waitangi. Such intermarriages often helped to establish a kinship network which was the basis of the settlements. Many of these existed up the Waitangi River as far inland as Lake Owhareiti.

Although it is now difficult to establish the facts with certainty, archeological evidence indicates that some Maori settlements in the Waitangi area might not have been occupied all year round. South of the Treaty House on the level land where the Waitangi Hotel now stands, middens and garden sites have been identified and it is most likely that around here a pa would have been situated. Other middens have been found stretching along Hutia Creek and the banks of the Waitangi River up as far as the Haruru Falls. In all probability the inland hapu annually migrated to the sea for a three month period during which they fished and gathered shell-fish.

The Ngapuhi struggle for supremacy during the latter years of the eighteenth century and the early years of the nineteenth caused constant inter-tribal turmoil in the Bay of Islands and its interior. Ngapuhi military expeditions against other tribal groups often resulted in the forced movement of peoples who harboured a lasting resentment of such treatment. Once lives were taken and enmities established members of a rival tribe demanded **utu** or revenge.

Yet the Ngapuhi themselves were sometimes threatened by invaders from the south. In about 1793 the Ngati Maru people of Waitemata had actually attacked the Ngapuhi stronghold at Puketona. This they reached by travelling undetected inland up the river from Waitangi. Obviously Waitangi could not have been in Ngapuhi hands at the time and indeed did not become so until well into the new century. It was from the Ngatipou that in May 1815 the missionaries William Hall and Thomas Kendall purchased fifty acres of land at Waitangi from Waraki, the Ngatipou chief, for the sum of five axes.

Although Ngapuhi pressure made Waraki's hold on Waitangi extremely tenuous, a bloodless Ngapuhi takeover was finally achieved by the marriage of Ruatara to Waraki's daughter. Yet even this event did not bring immediate peace and security to the area.

1769—FIRST EUROPEAN CONTACTS

The first Europeans seen by Maori of the Bay of Islands were explorers. On 27 November 1769 Lieutenant James Cook recorded in his log that the *Endeavour* had come abreast of a great cape. At its tip was Motukokako, the pierced rock which marks the end of the cape Rakaumangamanga, which Cook re-named for Sir Piercy Brett, the distinguished Lord of the Admiralty who had signed the secret orders authorising Cook to explore the southern ocean after having observed the transit of Venus. It is testimony to Cook's punning sense of humour that he chose to record his patron's unusual Christian name in calling the rock Piercy Island, while reserving his surname for Cape Brett.

Piercy Island, formerly Motukokako, was re-named by Cook.

11

At Matauri Bay Cook found small islands populated with fortified villages belonging to Ngapuhi from Hokianga who had already gained a foothold there. Here he met with the chief Tapua who, with his young son Patuone, boarded the *Endeavour* from the canoe Te Tumuaki. Cook described how over three hundred natives assembled in their canoes around his ship and how he gave one chief a piece of cloth and distributed a few nails among others.

Cook spent a week in the Bay of Islands making a map outline of the more accessible areas of the inner harbour of the south east side of the Bay. Again at Motu Arohia, now known as Roberton Island, canoes swarmed around the *Endeavour.* When she launched a pinnace for the purpose of taking soundings Maori tried to board the small boat by force. Attempts were also made to steal an anchor and Cook had to fire one of the ship's guns to discourage the act. He had to resort to the same device when attempts were made to remove several of his boats which had gone ashore on Motu Arohia to inspect the cultivations. Maori were observed to be quite unperturbed by musket fire but apparently became "as meek as lambs" upon the firing of the ship's guns.

By the time Cook sailed away on Wednesday December 6th 1769 he had formed a favourable impression of the Bay of Islands, as he had named it.
" It affords," he wrote "a good anchorage and every kind of refreshment for shipping."

1772—MARION DU FRESNE'S EXPEDITION

It was to be over two years before Maori saw Europeans again. On 3 May 1772 two French ships approached Cape Brett. These were the *Mascarin* under the command of M. Marc-Joseph Marion du Fresne and its store ship, the *Marquis de Castries* under the twenty-two year old M. Ambroise du Clesmeur. They were sailing from the island of Mauritius to Tahiti with the purpose of returning to his home Ahu-Toru, a native Tahitian who had been taken to France in 1769 by the navigator Bougainville.

Marion du Fresne, at the age of 47 had a distinguished naval career behind him. Wealthy and idealistic, he welcomed the opportunity for adventure. He had managed to secure two government vessels by guaranteeing to pay all the expenses of the voyage including the crew's wages. The passage around the Cape of Good Hope had been uneventful but by the time the two ships arrived at the Bay of Islands they had been battered by storms at sea and were dangerously short of fresh water and food. Not surprisingly many of the crew were ill with scurvy and unable to walk. Du Fresne's expedition had left Mauritius in October 1771, before news of Cook's voyage had been reported, so it was merely coincidental that they should have arrived on May 4 1772 at the very spot which Cook had declared so advantageous for refreshment. Du Clesmeur described in his diary how once again Maori fearlessly approached their vessels in their canoes, but no one would come on board until enticed with gifts. When a group of them eventually did board the *Mascarin,* du Fresne dressed them in shirts and breeches " but they had no sooner left the ship than they divested themselves of these new clothes to put their own back on."

As a result of such generosity many more Maori were encouraged and, wrote du Clesmeur, " finally we had on board at least a hundred New Zealanders, who sang and danced almost all the time, and it was only with difficulty that we got rid of them, and even then on condition that we would pay them a visit. To engage us still further they gave us to understand that their women were pretty, hoping to attract us by this ploy which is indeed an effective way to unite nations the most disparate in their ways, their manners and their customs."

Fresh potatoes and fish were sold to the ships; a camp for care of the sick sailors was set up at Waipao on the south west side of Moturua Island; the ships were cleaned and parties sent inland to search for timber which might be suitable for spars, Maori helping to drag the logs overland. Many pleasant excursions to other parts of the Bay were made. One day the *Mascarin's* longboat rounded Tapeka Point and sailed to the south west side of the Bay where in a small cove, either at or very near Waitangi, oysters were found. There were many such expeditions because du Fresne was particularly fond of the shellfish.

Extremely friendly relationships were established with Maori, du Clesmeur writing that " we led the gentlest, happiest life that one could hope for among savage peoples. They traded their fish and their game with us with the greatest good faith, and our sailors far from being discouraged by the rigours of winter and heavy work, gave us each day fresh proof of their zeal so that we imagined that we would soon be seaworthy again."

So trusting were Maori of their unexpected guests that chiefs showed delight at being permitted to sleep on board the two French ships. Du Fresne's contacts with the chief Te Kauri resulted in daily contact with members of his people, the Te Hikutu. Sailors visited his fortified pa; below it, du Fresne calmly went on afternoon walks and fishing expeditions to bays out of sight of his own camp.

When things began to go missing du Fresne explained to his men that Maori had no concept of ownership. He was annoyed when his men tied a Ngati Pou chief, Rawhi, to a stake in order to force him to confess to the stealing of a musket. Du Fresne ordered the man's immediate release and gave instructions that a better watch should be kept in future. Du Clesmeur, like others, was at a loss to understand his commander's Rousseauian belief in the essential goodness of the New Zealanders and wrote with exasperation of du Fresne's utterly blind trust in them. Du Fresne remained adamant that his men should do no harm to any Maori.

Despite his romantic ideals about Maori as Noble Savages, the expedition was to have a tragic conclusion. Groups of sailors going about their work gradually began to notice slight changes in the demeanour of Maori. The tieing up of a chief had been a singularly stupid act and no doubt caused ill-feeling among Maori who would undoubtedly have regarded it as a gross offence against the mana of a high ranking chief. The *Mascarin's* Lieutenant Jean Roux recalled his suspicion of the chief Te Kauri's intense interest in everything the French sailors did but, despite du Fresne's often-stated belief in his sincerity, those under his command were increasingly unable to believe in or convey similar messages of trust to their hosts.

In another similar incident, du Fresne himself briefly chained a Maori who attempted to remove a cutlass by escaping through a porthole in the ship's gunroom. Later a group of French officers aggravated the increasingly tense situation by stealing a magnificent seventy foot long canoe which they found beached and unwisely took, believing it to be abandoned.

The nervous French began to threaten groups of Maori with musket fire and soon trust between the two was broken. Gradually Maori became less willing to enter the French camps though they did continue their helpfulness to isolated individuals who became lost in the bush. It even became necessary for those watching the hospital camp to erect blunderbusses so that sentries could be ready in the event of a visit by Maori intent on more than mere theft. Lieutenant Roux, in particular, was worried and told du Fresne of his fears. In reply du Fresne described to him how a few days earlier he had been led ashore by a group of chiefs who invited him to climb a mountain near Te Kauri's village.

" On this mountain," reported Roux, "there were many people and they made him sit down along with the officers who were with him. He received many caresses from them, then they put a sort of crown of feathers on his head, showing him the whole expanse of the land and making him understand that they recognised him as their king . . . for his part he also gave them many presents and caresses and they escorted him back on board ship. After telling me this Mr Marion said to me: "How can you expect me to have a poor opinion of a people who show so much friendship for me? Since I do them nothing but good, surely they will not do me any harm."

On the bright moonlit night of 12 June there was a great deal of movement in the bush around the French hospital camp on Moturua Island as Maori crouched in the fern in order to inspect the newly installed defensive weaponry. At dawn Roux, the officer in charge, saw that the surrounding mountains were swarming with armed Maori. Then a lone unarmed chief already known to Roux advanced, crying and uttering the words " Tacoury maté Marion" which meant Te Kauri has killed Marion.

The previous day du Fresne had gone ashore at two o'clock in the afternoon with a group of chiefs who had come to fetch him for a hunting and fishing expedition. He had taken sixteen men but refused the company of soldiers. Before he had disembarked a Maori had thrown himself at his feet weeping and telling du Fresne that if he went ashore Te Kauri would surely kill him. Du Fresne's men in turn begged their commander to pay attention to the warning but du Fresne brushed it aside.

That night, although they failed to return, there was no alarm because du Fresne had often slept ashore. Next morning the *Castries'* long boat went ashore as usual, its men travelling inland some distance to cut wood. Later those remaining on board the ship noticed a man swimming back out to the ship. He had been wounded by a spear blow in the thigh and described how he had seen his companions hacked to pieces with their own axes. This survivor, Yves Thomas, managed to flee, catching sight of du Fresne's empty boat beached at a cove as he did so. Roux, hearing this tale, knew immediately that the chief who had come to him had spoken the truth.

In the days which followed the French saw Maori flaunting du Fresne's velvet jacket and silver-mounted musket. They cried out that they had " killed Marion" and brandished their clubs to demonstrate how. Roux led a vengeful attack on the pa at Paeroa. Later he destroyed Te Kauri's now deserted pa having found cooked human bones with pieces of flesh still adhering to them— clear evidence that du Fresne and his men had been killed and eaten. Te Kauri himself was shot and wounded.

Death of Marion du Fresne
Charles Meryon (1821-1868)
Crayon, pencil and chalk drawing (1848)
ALEXANDER TURNBULL LIBRARY

The artist studied drawing at the Brest Naval School before embarking on the Rhin for a four-year voyage 1842-46 to the southern ocean. Drawn after his return to France, Meryon's picture transformed du Fresne's death into an heroic event.

The French, now continually armed and ready for any attack, hastened their preparations to leave New Zealand. The work bringing the masts out of the bush was only partially accomplished and with difficulty; the scurvy sufferers had to be brought back on board from the hospital camp on Moturua; some of the ship's boats had to be left behind. Roux described scathingly how M. Crozet, who now took command, fired several useless cannon shots at Te Kauri's lower village.

On 12 July 1772 the *Mascarin* and the *Marquis de Castries* sailed away from Moturoa with the loss of their leader and twenty six others. They had killed many Maori in reprisal for du Fresne's death. Before leaving they renamed Moturua Marion Island; at Waipao they buried a bottle containing the arms of the kingdom they proclaimed as La France Australe, or Southern France. It has never been found.

In 1991, Anne Salmond revealed in her book **Two Worlds** that Maori accounts of du Fresne's visit made it clear that his men had violated a tapu. It appeared they had fished in a bay in which some of Te Kauri's Te Hikutu people had earlier drowned. Dr Salmond wrote that, "the fish of the bay had been touched by the tapu of death, and had themselves perhaps been nibbled on the bodies of the drowned men. To catch these fish was bad enough but to eat them was tantamount to cannibalism, an attack on the tapu of corpses and that of their tribe, and on the mana of their tribal gods."

It is also likely that Maori came to believe that the French would never leave. Once they understood the power of the firearms they had every cause to fear the relaxed pace of du Fresne's visit. It is probable that having killed the French commander they thought that his followers would quickly disperse and in that belief they were undoubtedly proved right.

Events of this kind were to have a profound effect on the future relationship between Maori of different tribes as well as between Maori and Pakeha. Maori were left in no doubt as to the power of the musket and its relevance to their warlike way of life. Already involved in a power struggle between rival tribes which was to result in the eventual superiority of the Ngapuhi people, they were only too ready to appropriate those aspects of "civilisation" which the next European visitors to their shores would bring. Their experience with the French had taught them that guests were to be treated with caution. When the first missionaries and whalers arrived they came among a people already conditioned by earlier experience not only to be suspicious but also eager to make use of any benefits the newcomers brought.

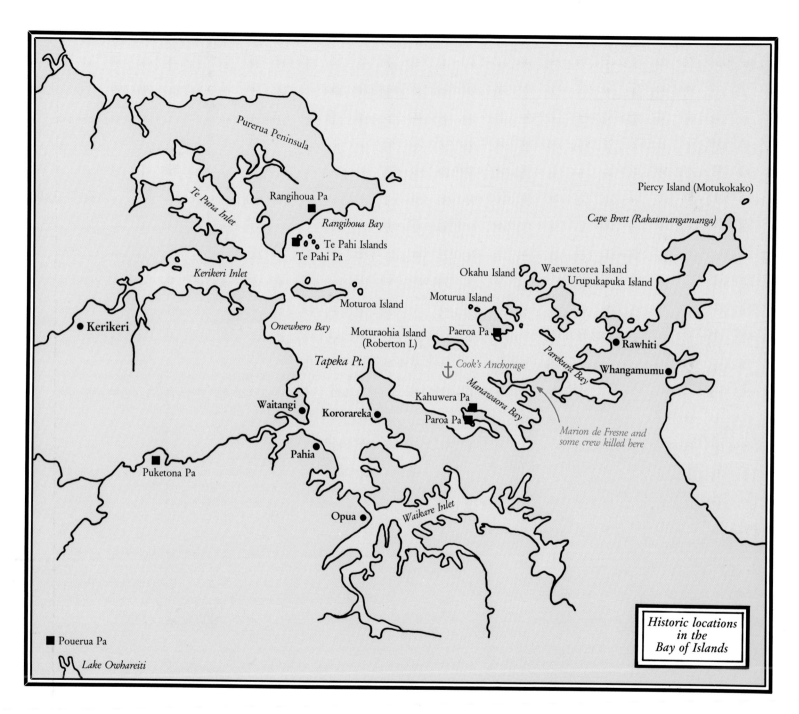

Purerua Peninsula

Te Puna Inlet

Rangihoua Pa

Rangihoua Bay

Te Pahi Islands
Te Pahi Pa

Kerikeri Inlet

Moturoa Island

● **Kerikeri**

Onewhero Bay

Moturaohia Island
(Roberton I.)

Tapeka Pt.

Okahu Island

Waewaetorea Island
Urupukapuka Island

Moturua Island

Paeroa Pa

Piercy Island (Motukokako)

Cape Brett (Rakaumangamanga)

● **Rawhiti**

Parekura Bay

⚓ Cook's Anchorage

Manawaora Bay

Whangamumu ●

Waitangi

Kororareka ●

Kahuwera Pa

Paroa Pa

Marion de Fresne and
some crew killed here

Pahia ●

Puketona Pa

Opua ●

Waikare Inlet

■ Pouerua Pa

Lake Owhareiti

*Historic locations
in the
Bay of Islands*

Sydney Cove in 1801 from The Early History of New Zealand
Sherrin and Wallace, Auckland 1890
AUCKLAND MUSEUM

Rangihu: the Rev. Samuel Marsden's cottage at Parramatta
Sketched by the Rev. Richard Taylor in 1836.

Marsden named his Sydney house "Rangihu"after the bay where he
had established New Zealand's first mission.
Sherrin and Wallace 1890
AUCKLAND MUSEUM

WHALERS AND SEALERS

Although both Cook and du Fresne had claimed New Zealand for their respective sovereigns neither government took any immediate interest. The situation changed in January 1778 with the establishment of the English convict settlement at Port Jackson, now Sydney. Although the first governor is said to have contemplated sending the most vicious criminals to New Zealand where they would with any luck be killed and eaten by cannibals, nothing of the kind took place.

Instead the most decisive influence on Maori was as a result of contact with whalers and sealers who had begun to work the waters around New Zealand. By 1805 the Bay of Islands had become a major whaling port; here ships could be refitted, supplies taken on and a vigorous trade in pork, vegetables, fish, spars promoted with Maori. In return the seamen bartered iron, clothes and muskets. There was an ever-increasing demand for the latter because of the tribal relocations which were taking place as the result of the gradual Ngapuhi takeover of the north.

Although there is evidence that whalers sometimes treated Maori very badly, a significant number became crew members of sealing and whaling vessels. One was the high ranking Ngapuhi chief called Ruatara, the same man who later married the daughter of Waraki of Waitangi. In 1805, at the age of 19, Ruatara left his home at Rangihoua as a crew member of the whaler, Argo. He spent the next four years serving on a number of whaling ships sometimes being well treated and at other times suffering beatings or near starvation.

In 1809 the missionary Samuel Marsden discovered Ruatara on board the convict ship Ann, bound for Australia. The chief had apparently managed to reach England where he was disappointed at being unable to see King George III. Now extremely ill he was vomiting blood because of the severity of beatings he had received from his fellow crew members. Marsden rescued him and when they arrived at Port Jackson cared for him for eight months at his home at Parramatta. When Ruatara finally reached the Bay of Islands in 1812 he discovered that Te Puna, the island stronghold of the senior chief at Rangihoua, Te Pahi, had been attacked by the crews of five whaling ships and many of its inhabitants murdered.

The reasons for this terrible event lay in the rapid deterioration of relationships between visiting whalers and Maori between 1807 and 1812. Rangihoua Bay had been the centre of the trade between the two peoples not long before this. In 1805 Te Pahi made a visit to Port Jackson. There he and his four sons were accommodated at Government House by the Governor, Phillip King, who had seen the benefits of fostering friendly trading relations with the New

Zealanders. More importantly for the future, Te Pahi spent considerable time in the company of the missionary Samuel Marsden who was greatly impressed with his "clear, strong and comprehensive" mind. When Te Pahi left Port Jackson to return to New Zealand in February 1806 he was given iron tools, fruit tree seedlings, livestock and a small prefabricated house to build on his island at Te Puna. A plan drawn up to settle a group of official observers under his protection at Te Puna did not eventuate though the contact no doubt paved the way for Ruatara's later patronage of the Church Missionary Society at Rangihoua.

Unfortunately the relationship nurtured by Te Pahi's visit to Port Jackson came to nothing. Whalers had begun to abuse their trading obligations with Maori, often sailing away without paying for goods they had received. Maori crew members increasingly suffered the inhumane treatment Ruatara had received on board whaling ships. In 1813 it was even necessary for Governor Macquarie to issue a proclamation binding masters of ships to a rigid code of behaviour toward the native people of New Zealand and other Pacific islands.

It hardly came as a surprise when in 1808 Maori made the first attack on a European ship to have occurred since du Fresne's death in 1772. Maori evidence suggests that the schooner *Parramatta* had arrived in the Bay in distress and had been supplied with food and water. When payment was demanded Maori on board were simply shot or thrown overboard. Unfortunately for those who might have imagined that they could sail away unscathed following such acts, fierce winds drove the ship ashore and there the entire crew was set upon and killed.

Later, in mid-1808 a Captain Ceroni of the sealing ship *Commerce* sought to obtain supplies at Te Puna. Te Pahi advised him to go instead to the Whangaroa Harbour thirty kilometres to the north of the Bay of Islands where Te Pahi's kinsman Kaitoke would oblige with the necessary supplies. Te Pahi travelled with the ship to Whangaroa and further to its destination of Port Jackson. However, when Ceroni appeared again the following year on board the *City of Edinburgh* Te Pahi flatly refused to give him any assistance whatever.

The reason for his change of attitude was that he blamed Ceroni for his relative Kaitoke's death in an epidemic. On the previous visit Ceroni had dropped his watch, a source of great wonderment to Maori, into the sea at Whangaroa and terrified the spectators who considered that it contained an **atua**. Because the epidemic was attributed to this act Ceroni had to go to across the bay to Kororareka for supplies.

With the formerly friendly Maori at Te Puna and Whangaroa now disaffected it was apparent that the situation was getting out of hand. In 1810 the schoone *Boyd* returned Te Ara, a sealer and brother of the Ngapuhi chief Te Puhi, to Whangaroa. During the *Boyd's* voyage across the Tasman its captain had Te Ara flogged and when the *Boyd* arrived at Whangaroa inflicted more

Te Pahi, the senior chief at Rangihoua, travelled to Sydney where he was befriended by Europeans eager to trade with Maori in the Bay of Islands. Sherrin and Wallace 1890
AUCKLAND MUSEUM

19

Whangaroa Harbour showing the position of the Boyd before it was attacked.
Sherrin and Wallace 1890
AUCKLAND MUSEUM

Upper Whangaroa Harbour showing where the Boyd drifted after taking fire.
Sherrin and Wallace 1890
AUCKLAND MUSEUM

floggings on Maori crew members. Such insults could not go unavenged and so Captain Thompson and some members of his crew were led inland in search of good timber for spars and killed. Later the *Boyd* was attacked and its crew slaughtered. During the celebration which followed there was an explosion and the ship drifted up the harbour on fire. Unfortunately the blame for the burning and massacre fell on Te Pahi who, although he probably had some minor involvement, was not responsible.

Reprisals swiftly followed and Ruatara was to discover on his return home in 1812 that Te Puna was burnt to the ground. The vengeance-minded whalers had probably confused Te Ara's brother Te Puhi's name with that of Te Pahi. The major piece of incriminating evidence was that a longboat and clothing from the *Boyd* were found at Te Puna. The *Boyd* tragedy marked the climax of a period of increasing hostility between Maori and pakeha. Fewer ships called and it was not until 1814 with the arrival of Samuel Marsden and the missionaries of the Church Missionary Society that trade was fully restored.

The Burning of the Boyd, Whangaroa Harbour
Walter Wright (1866-1933) Oil on canvas (1908)
AUCKLAND CITY ART GALLERY

A New Zealand artist sees a dramatic moment in his country's history through the eyes of the great English painter J. M. W. Turner.

THE MISSIONARIES AT RANGIHOUA

On Christmas Day 1814 Reverend Samuel Marsden preached the first Christian sermon ever delivered in New Zealand at the far end of the idyllic beach at Oihi now known as Marsden Cross. Here, where a small stream flowed below Ruatara's huge pa of Rangihoua, Maori and Pakeha gathered to listen. The spot had been chosen because of its proximity to Marsden's reliable but ailing patron's pa. Ruatara had planted a Union Jack as a welcoming gesture; the congregation of missionaries and their families, some convicts, and Maori from both sides of the Bay listened quietly. When Marsden finished three hundred warriors danced a haka around him.

Marsden had long been determined to set up a mission station under the auspices of the Church Missionary Society in New Zealand. In 1814 he had purchased the brig *Active* to carry out an exploratory journey to the Bay of Islands. Two missionaries on board, Thomas Kendall and William Hall, were to find out at first hand how Maori would receive the idea of a European settlement. Ruatara was by this time experienced in European ways, farming European-style on the island of Moturata; European clothing was worn and European food eaten. Hall and Kendall also reported to Marsden that Tara, the old chief at Kororareka, and Hongi Hika of Kerikeri were well disposed to the idea of a mission. Probably Hongi quite accurately foresaw the possibility of European firearms in his plans for Ngapuhi supremacy. Settlers, whether missionaries or not, were dependant upon Maori support for their survival in this isolated place; trade in muskets was bound to flourish as a means of payment for land and initial supplies.

Marsden Cross, erected to commemorate the establishment of the mission at Rangihoua in 1814.

Rangihoua pa from the walking track which leads down to the bay where Marsden landed. Terracing on the pa site is still clearly visible.

Landing of Revd. Samuel Marsden in New Zealand, December 1814 Samuel Williams (1788-1853) Engraved in 1847 and published in the Annals of the Diocese of New Zealand.
ALEXANDER TURNBULL LIBRARY

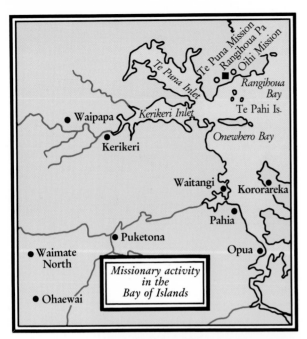

Missionary activity in the Bay of Islands

With Marsden's blessing Hall and Kendall returned to Sydney in July 1814 accompanied by Ruatara, Hongi Hika and his son Korokoro. They set sail again on 19 November 1814 under Captain Hansen to set up the mission at Rangihoua.

Marsden's ideas about the mission were unusual. Its Christian nature would emerge, he believed, as missionaries and natives went about their practical work together. He was convinced that the blessings of civilisation had first to be established in the minds of the native people in order to make them receptive to the message of salvation. The schoolteacher Kendall, Hall, the carpenter and John King, the shoemaker, were chosen by the CMS as much for their practical abilities as their religious conviction. Judith Binney points out that they had been given no training, were ill-educated, and certainly had little idea of the difficulties they would have to face. After Marsden left for Australia, Kendall, Hall and King began to squabble among themselves, mainly because Kendall's appointment as a Justice of the Peace in the Bay of Islands was resented by others offended by his apparently superior manner and his incautious exercise of authority. The tensions of physical isolation were great. Bitter quarrels erupted between the men of God.

The Missionary Settlement at Rangihoua
Oil on wood panel (ca. 1832) Artist Unknown
REX NAN KIVELL COLLECTION,
NATIONAL LIBRARY OF AUSTRALIA

Portrait of Samuel Marsden,
Richard Read (attrib.)
Pencil and wash on card. (1833)
ALEXANDER TURNBULL LIBRARY

To make matters worse, Ruatara, the missionaries' main protector, became less and less enthusiastic about his introduction of Europeans. After Marsden left he withdrew his active support thus increasing the sense of isolation felt by the missionaries. Then he became seriously ill and on 3 March 1815 he died. With him died the scheme which he and Marsden had planned for a European town built at Te Puna to the immediate west of Rangihoua. In an impossible position, the missionaries were now unable to support themselves because the hills at Rangihoua were so steep and the soil so shallow that successful cultivation was very difficult. Despite Hongi Hika's assurances that he would take up Ruatara's protective role, the missionaries felt increasingly vulnerable at their settlement below Rangihoua pa.

Hongi Hongi Hongi Hika
George French Angas (1822-1886)
Hand-coloured tinted lithograph (1847)
Published in **The New Zealanders Illustrated**, London 1847
ALEXANDER TURNBULL LIBRARY

Habitants de la Nouvelle-Zélande avec une vue de leur place fortifiée ou Hippah
(Inhabitants of New Zealand with a view of their fortified stronghold or Hippah).
Antoine Chazal after Francois-Louis Lejeune (1804-1851)
Drawing, pencil and watercolour (1825-26)
ALEXANDER TURNBULL LIBRARY

This view of Rangihoua pa was originally the work of the eighteen year-old Lejeune, a member of Duperrey's 1822-25 expedition on board the *Coquille*. Chazal (1793-1854) was a painter and engraver.

View north from Waitangi towards Kerikeri Inlet.

A MISSION AT WAITANGI PROPOSED

Contrary to Marsden's instructions Kendall and Hall decided that it was time to move the mission station. Their choice of a new location fell on the flat land at Waitangi. In a letter dated July 6 1815 Kendall described his actions to Marsden: "Went over the bay to Whitangi in company with Mr Hall where we met with the chief Warrakkee and purchased off him a parcel of land for the Society containing by Admeasurement fifty acres being the most eligible spot in the Bay of Islands for settlement. Warrakkee expressed, as several other native chiefs had done, his fears that the English should in a little time increase their force and drive the Natives into the Bush and take away their land from them. We endeavoured to convince him to the contrary. He replied to our observations "that it was good for a few white people to live at New Zealand but not for so many."

Despite his doubts, Waraki accepted the payment of five axes for fifty acres of his land. In July Hall went across to Waitangi with two convict sawyers, Conroy and Campbell, to build a house for his family. It was sited in the gully which today bears his name. Timber from Kawakawa was more easily accessible at Waitangi than it had been from Rangihoua and work proceeded smoothly. On 5 September Mr and Mrs Hall and their baby daughter, one of the first Europeans born in New Zealand, went to live there—against Marsden's advice.

During the time their house at Waitangi was being built the old Ngatipou chief Waraki died. For many years he had successfully resisted pressure from the advancing Ngapuhi. Now a number of **taua muru** or plundering raids began. The first, on 24 June 1815, actually occured while the Waitangi people were attending the **tangi** of their chief Waraki. The convict sawyer Conroy, the lone European at Waitangi, was also attacked and Kendall, whose relationship with Hall had deteriorated, used this as an excuse to remain at Rangihoua rather than go forward with his plan to move the mission to Waitangi.

Despite the unsettled situation Hall was at first enthusiastic about his new home. He established a vegetable garden with such success that he described Waitangi as "the garden of New Zealand." But he had difficulties when Maori employed as agricultural labourers constantly stole his tools despite the fact that he paid them for their work with axes and other implements. Then on 25 January 1816 a Ngapuhi taua muru from Whangamumu on the eastern side of the Bay arrived at Waitangi to avenge themselves on Waraki's people for alleged disrespect to a sacred relic. Hall's house was plundered and everything removable taken away. The missionary described how he attempted to defend his property . . . "They immediately laid hold of me and threw me down and got upon me and brandished their war instruments over me—it could be nothing but some Almighty power that saved Daniel out of the jaws of the Lions that delivered me out of the hands of these savages—And when Mrs Hall saw me seized she came running towards me and a native met her and struck her in the face with a war instrument and knocked her down, and when I got myself wrested out from under them I beheld my dear partner laying moaning and I could not see a feature in her face for blood."

The blow permanently impaired her sight. Only the arrival of the local Ngatipou prevented further damage. On hearing of the incident the ship *Catherine* under Captain Graham sailed from Paroa Bay north of Kororareka and the Hall family was returned to Rangihoua. Although their house was dismantled and rebuilt at Rangihoua, Hall continued to travel to Waitangi to tend his wheat and barley cultivation which he maintained until 1824 when he returned to England.

Meanwhile there had been further developments in the struggle for control of the Bay. Ngapuhi invaders from the eastern side of the Bay had gradually evicted all remnant Ngatiawa hapu. By 1820 under their chief Kaiteke they had displaced the Ngati Rahiri hapu of Ngapuhi which had occupied Waitangi between 1815-19. Certainly it was Ngapuhi inhabitants of Waitangi who in 1822 rescued a sailor who survived the destruction of the *Vansi Hart,* a ship which foundered on the rocks on the shore at Waitangi in heavy seas.

There had been further developments among the missionaries too. In 1823 Marsden returned to Waitangi accompanied by the missionary Henry Williams with the aim of setting up a mission station at Waitangi. By this time he had overcome his earlier objections to a mission sited anywhere but Rangihoua and in 1819 he had purchased 13,000 acres from Hongi Hika at Kerikeri. The proposed mission at Waitangi would have been the CMS's third following those at Te Puna and Kerikeri.

Marsden described his visit to Waitangi in his journal for August 5 1823: "We had some conversation with the inhabitants on the subject and told them what our intentions were, but could come to no arrangements with them as the principal chiefs were absent at the wars. We crossed the Wythangee River and examined the ground upon the opposite side, which appeared very good also. There is a large population at both of these places and a number of very fine children, who continually surround us. The head chief of the place was also gone to the wars, so that we could not come to any final determination this day and therefore returned on board in the evening."

Hutia Creek from Hall's Gully

Rangihoua, a New Zealand fortified village, the residence of Wharepoaka (1827)
Augustus Earle (1793-1838)
REX NAN KIVELL COLLECTION
NATIONAL LIBRARY of AUSTRALIA

THE NGAPUHI WARS

The phrase "gone to the wars" used by Marsden is a reference to the bloody tribal wars which had in fact been fought since 1814. Initiated by Ngapuhi they reached a peak of violence in the period 1818-24 under the leadership of the chiefs Hongi Hika and Te Morenga. During these years large Ngapuhi raiding parties, sometimes in alliance with local tribes, terrorised the people of Hauraki, Kawhia, Taranaki and travelled as far south as Wellington. Ngapuhi were understandably dreaded by southern tribes who did not have access to firearms and could only resort to hand to hand fighting. They traded with whalers for arms and increasingly with the missionaries who now found that hoes, axes, nails and blankets were less desirable to Maori in exchange for food. A steady growth in the European population had ensured that the Bay of Islands became New Zealand's centre of trade with Europeans during the 1820s. Maori were prepared to work hard if they could be guaranteed payment in muskets. Traders too realised that there was money to be made in serving the needs of the whalers using Kororareka as a main base of operations. Now the missionaries found themselves in a minority and in the face of the immorality of visiting crews they struggled in vain to preserve a continued Maori respect for European civilised values. Missionaries themselves even became involved in the distasteful trade in preserved Maori heads, a practice only finally outlawed in 1831 by order of Governor Darling of New South Wales.

The most compromised of all the missionaries was Thomas Kendall. He not only traded muskets with Maori but also for a period in 1821 lived with a Maori servant named Tungaroa, daughter of the chief Rakau of Rangihoua. Already estranged from his wife Jane, Kendall had travelled to England the previous year with the aim of being ordained an Anglican priest. With him on board the New Zealander were Hongi Hika and the young Rangihoua chief, Waikato, both of whom undertook the journey to obtain further supplies of arms.

They were introduced to George III who presented Hongi Hika with a suit of armour which he later wore in battle. Kendall, although strongly censured by the CMS for his trade in muskets, continued the practice upon his return to New Zealand. Hongi immediately began assembling a massive war party and began a rampage through the North Island. In September 1821 he set off to attack Ngati Paoa strongholds at Panmure, Auckland, returning in triumph bearing the head of the Ngati Paoa chief, Te Hinaki. In March 1822 another large party of warriors descended on the Ngati Maru pa at Te Totara, Thames, killing over one thousand people.

Hongi Hika, after Ruatara's death the appointed Maori protector of the missionaries at Rangihoua, was now an embarrassment to Marsden. The Maori

The Revd. Thomas Kendall and the Maori chiefs Hongi Hika and Waikato
James Barry Oil (1820)
ALEXANDER TURNBULL LIBRARY

military leader already disapproved of Marsden's condemnation of his friend Kendall's activities as a seller of muskets. Hongi Hika was further disappointed when he heard that a new appointment to the mission, George Clarke, a gunsmith, would be employed as a catechist and schoolmaster rather than as an armourer.

But after 1826 Hongi Hika was a spent force. He apparently never recovered from the death in battle of his son Hare Hongi in 1825. Plagued by ill health he lost the use of an arm and had several times to be persuaded against suicide. In December 1826 he finally left his pa of Okuratope at Waimate in favour of Whangaroa where he intended to punish the local people for disrupting the life of the Wesleyan Mission. Always eager to encourage trade between Maori and pakeha it was his intention to see that nothing should disrupt commerce there. When his war party reached Whangaroa Hongi Hika was wounded in the chest by a ball fired from a musket, the weapon for whose introduction he more than any other had been responsible. He was not to die for some months, in March 1828, and his death was kept secret for fear of reprisals against the missionaries at Kerikeri whom he had protected for so long.

Habitants de la Nouvelle Zélande
(Inhabitants of New Zealand)
Antoine Chazal after Francois-Louis Lejeune (1826)
ALEXANDER TURNBULL LIBRARY
Hongi Hika, chief of Kerikeri is shown wearing a greenstone mere over one arm.

Distant View of the Bay of Islands, New Zealand. (1827)
Augustus Earle (1793-1838)
REX NAN KIVELL COLLECTION, NATIONAL LIBRARY OF AUSTRALIA
A lone sun-hatted European accompanied by Maori bearers surveys the impressively romantic panorama.

MISSIONARIES, SETTLERS AND LAND SALES

Établissement des Missionaires (Nouvelle Zélande)
(Missionaries' station (New Zealand)   1828-1833
J. Arago after Louis-Auguste de Sainson
ALEXANDER TURNBULL LIBRARY

De Sainson visited Paihia, home of the Revd. Henry Williams and his family on 12 March 1827, the first day of the Astrolabe's visit to the Bay of Islands.

Because in 1823 Marsden had been unable to negotiate a land sale at Waitangi while Kaiteke was away with one of Hongi Hika's war parties, he decided to establish the missionary Henry Williams at Paihia instead. For the second time Waitangi was passed over as a site of missionary activity in the Bay of Islands. Although the name Marsden Vale failed to replace the Maori Paihia, the mission prospered and by 1830 had become the Church Missionary Society's principal establishment.

In 1826 of the pioneer missionaries only John King remained at Te Puna, as the original mission behind Rangihoua was now generally known. The mission at Kerikeri was maintained by the families of James Kemp, George Clarke, James Hamlin and from 1828 by the Revd. William Yate. In 1830 when the inland mission at Waimate was established following the purchase of land by Marsden, the missionaries Clarke, Hamlin and Yate moved there.

Now Maori began to sell land to individual settlers; previously their land sales had been almost exclusively with missionaries. These sales to resident traders were enthusiastically pursued on both sides; the Maori had an insatiable appetite for European made goods and the traders, who now arrived in increasing numbers, were keen to buy their own plots of land as cheaply as possible.

William Yate recorded in his 'An Account of New Zealand' (1835) that by 1834 there were one thousand permanent European settlers in the Bay. The earlier barter economy gradually gave way to a cash one, mainly involving British and American currencies. Among the earliest traders were Gilbert Mair, the kauri gum exporter and shipping agent of Te Wahapu and Joel Samuel Polack, the flax and timber trader and land speculator of Kororareka. In 1833 the first resident doctor arrived. He was Dr Ross, who bought land at Waitangi and lived there briefly in two locations but following difficulties with Maori preferred to live at the mission at Paihia.

Although Maori themselves pursued sales of their land to Europeans it was not long before apprehension about the arrival of large numbers of additional Europeans in the Bay of Islands was felt. Middle class trading European settlers were also increasingly concerned about the issue of law and order in the settlement at Kororareka once brothels and grog shops were established there to service the needs of ships' crews. The missionaries too felt increasingly uneasy as racial tensions grew and immorality threatened their ability to promote decent Christian behaviour as an example to Maori.

Plage de Kororareka (Kororareka Beach)
Sigismond Himely, after Barthelemy Lauvergne
(1805-1871)
Aquatint
ALEXANDER TURNBULL LIBRARY

An image of friendly conversational exchange between Maori and European.

A LETTER TO THE KING

In October 1831 the first political crisis that was eventually to lead to the signing of the Treaty of Waitangi in 1840 took place. A French vessel, the heavily armed *La Favorite,* arrived in the Bay. Its commander, Captain Laplace, had in his charge a crew many of whom were ill, as du Fresne's had been. There had already been rumours in New South Wales that Laplace intended to claim New Zealand for France as the survivors of du Fresne's expedition were alleged to have done in 1782. It was also suggested that he had come to avenge the deaths of du Fresne and his men. Whatever the truth of these rumours, their possible consequences were apparent to the missionaries. Led by Revd. William Yate they induced thirteen chiefs to sign a letter to King William IV asking that he should extend his protection to New Zealand. It was no doubt confirming of their fears that *La Favorite* should anchor in the Bay the very day after the signing of the letter.

It is possible to view this document with a degree of scepticism. The names of influential chiefs were missing yet the letter sounds as though the signatories represented the whole country. The letter undoubtedly reflects more about missionary anxiety over the growing disruption of life in the Bay than it does about specifically Maori concerns. But evidently Lord Goderich at the Colonial Office in London did not think so. It was this letter more than anything else which was to be the catalyst for the appointment of a British Resident domiciled at Waitangi in 1833.

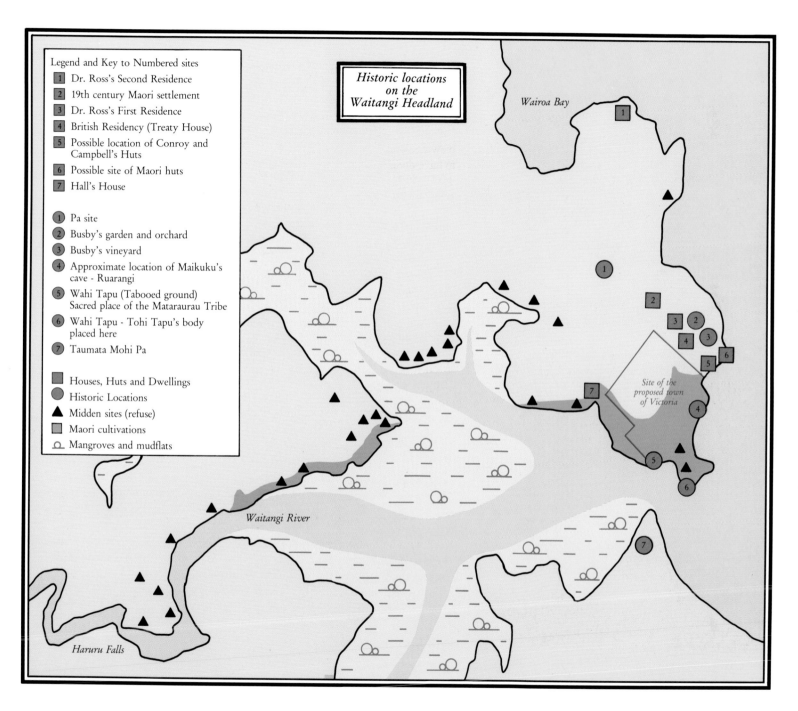

Legend and Key to Numbered sites

▢1 Dr. Ross's Second Residence
▢2 19th century Maori settlement
▢3 Dr. Ross's First Residence
▢4 British Residency (Treaty House)
▢5 Possible location of Conroy and Campbell's Huts
▢6 Possible site of Maori huts
▢7 Hall's House

①1 Pa site
②2 Busby's garden and orchard
③3 Busby's vineyard
④4 Approximate location of Maikuku's cave - Ruarangi
⑤5 Wahi Tapu (Tabooed ground) Sacred place of the Mataraurau Tribe
⑥6 Wahi Tapu - Tohi Tapu's body placed here
⑦7 Taumata Mohi Pa

▣ Houses, Huts and Dwellings
⬤ Historic Locations
▲ Midden sites (refuse)
▢ Maori cultivations
☊ Mangroves and mudflats

Historic locations
on the
Waitangi Headland

Wairoa Bay

Site of the
proposed town
of Victoria

Waitangi River

Haruru Falls

A BRITISH RESIDENT

The Revd. Yate's letter was eventually received in London by the Secretary of State for the Colonies, Lord Goderich, who replied but did nothing immediately about the situation.

In February 1831 a twenty nine-year old viticulturalist, former orphanage superintendent and collector of internal revenue named James Busby (1802-1871) arrived in London from Sydney. He had spent seven years in the colony and was returning to England in the hope of advancing his career as a government employee in Australia. On the long sea voyage he busied himself by writing papers about viticulture, pauper immigration, the jury system and the state of New Zealand. These he delivered to the Colonial Office where he was initially rebuffed by being told that the Colonial Secretary would be very glad to employ him but was unable to state in what capacity.

By the time Busby left London to return to Australia he had, however, been appointed British Resident at the Bay of Islands. Lord Goderich was not unfamiliar with the problems in New Zealand which had been communicated to him during 1830-31 by Governor Darling of New South Wales who in turn had been informed by Marsden.

Busby's effective use of influential connections at home did not endear him to Governor Darling's successor in office, Governor Bourke, particularly as it was part of Lord Goderich's instructions to him that the colony of New South Wales was to pay Busby's salary of 500 pounds per annum and an additional 200 pounds for distribution as gifts to chiefs. Bourke was annoyed that Busby had corresponded directly with the Colonial Office and this probably explains his singular unhelpfulness to Busby once the Resident took up office at Waitangi.

When Busby returned to Sydney in October 1831 Bourke informed him in no uncertain terms about the limitations of the office of Resident. He was to protect well-disposed settlers and traders, to prevent outrages against Maori by Europeans and to apprehend escaped convicts. Although legislation was planned to empower the Resident to arrest and bring British subjects to trial in New South Wales for offences against British law, no such legislation was ever passed. Busby was a civilian and therefore not entitled to troops who might assist him to enforce law and order. Because New Zealand was an independent territory he could not be appointed a magistrate; neither had he any powers of arrest nor could he take sworn testimony. The British Resident was a powerless figurehead in an impossible position who could at best hope to be what Claudia Orange describes as a "a mediator in matters affecting British subjects alone, and a kind of race relations conciliator between Maori and Pakeha."

A HOUSE FOR THE RESIDENT

A Colonial Office minute dated 18 September 1833 precisely expresses the penny pinching official attitude to Busby's appointment: "Half salary is quite sufficient, and a house on a limited scale all that he can fairly expect. No constables or assistants to be sent with him."

The poor relationship between Governor Bourke and Busby was reflected in the clash which now occured over Busby's desire for a house which would reflect his status as British Resident. The missionaries William Hall and William Yate, who met Busby in Sydney during the period of preparation for his new position, told him that it would be well nigh impossible for him to construct a house of his own at the Bay of Islands. They also emphasised that it would be essential for the Resident to purchase land on which to build his house. Busby's solution to this problem was make the suggestion that he be supplied with a prefabricated house designed in Sydney which could be built for him by the carpenters on board the ship which delivered him to New Zealand.

With this plan in mind Busby contracted the colony's leading architect, John Verge, to design him a house suitable to his position both as Resident and also as husband of Agnes Dow whom he had married on 1 November 1832, just one month after arriving back in Sydney from England. Verge produced a design for a substantial house costing 592 pounds, 15 shillings and 4 pence which Governor Bourke flatly rejected as too expensive.

Acting on an instruction from England which declared that Busby was to be supplied only with the frame of a house rather than a complete one, Bourke next ordered the Colonial Architect, Ambrose Hallen, to redesign Verge's plan. Reduced to two small rooms with a passage which could be used as a third room if needed, the new design was to cost 278 pounds. To the Colonial Secretary he wrote, without a trace of irony, "I have the honour to state that a trifling alteration of the plan ... might be sufficient for immediate shelter." Outraged, Busby earnestly sought Bourke's reconsideration of the whole matter but the Governor remained firm. Hallen's modification of Verge's original design was to form the plan of the British Residency at Waitangi and the astonishingly basic beginnings of the Treaty House we know today.

Although the controversy over the type of house a married British Resident was to be provided with had been settled much to Busby's displeasure, there were further difficulties to overcome before he actually set sail for the Bay of Islands.

He was assigned to travel on board the *H.M. S. Imogene* but its master, Captain Price Blackwood, refused to carry the frame of the house on his ship, apparently because he considered it a security risk. To add insult to injury he

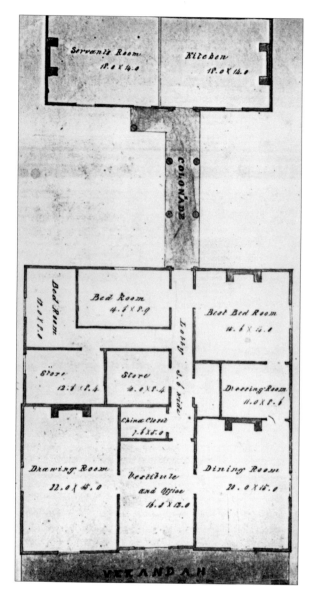

John Verge's original plan for a British Residency in New Zealand. MITCHELL LIBRARY

As the result of drastic alterations only the front rooms were built at Waitangi for James Busby.

James Busby painted by Sydney artist Richard Read on 12 September 1832. Read painted Agnes Dow shortly before she married Busby two months later. BUSBY FAMILY COLLECTION

refused to carry Busby's two horses and wrote to Governor Bourke insisting that Busby take as little luggage as possible.

On 21 April 1833 the *Imogene* sailed for New Zealand with James Busby on board bearing King William IV's reply to the Chiefs' letter. Busby arrived at the Bay on 4 May. It was not until the following month that the Residency's frame, bricks, weather boards, laths and roof shingles in Australian timbers with a quantity of Sydney sandstone for paving arrived on board the *New Zealander*. Busby's wife Agnes, preferring to wait until the house had been constructed, did not arrive until 28 July 1844, in the company of the Revd. William Yate on board the *Nereus*.

THE ARRIVAL OF HIS MAJESTY'S BRITISH RESIDENT

When the *Imogene* entered the Bay of Islands on Sunday 5 May 1833 the weather was so stormy and the seas so rough that it was impossible for Busby to land until the following Thursday. Meanwhile at Paihia the missionaries had invited Maori chiefs to assemble on 16 May to meet the King's representative and to hear what he had to communicate to them from the monarch.

The day began with a seven gun salute fired from *H.M.S. Imogene,* then Captain Blackwood and his officers accompanied James Busby ashore. On the beach they were greeted by Maori who fired muskets in the air and performed a haka. Busby was led to an enclosure in front of the Mission chapel where European settlers waited. He placed the King's letter on the table and the Revd. Henry Williams, speaking in Maori, proposed to the chiefs that Busby should read it. Officers and European settlers removed their hats to listen to the new Resident, speaking in English:

" The King is much gratified to find that the cause for alarm which appears to have existed at the time your letter was written has entirely passed away, and he trusts that no circumstances may occur in future to interrupt the internal tranquillity of New Zealand, which is so necessary to the maintenance of a close commercial intercourse between its inhabitants and those of Great Britain. The King is sorry for the injuries which you inform him the people of New Zealand have suffered from his subjects: but he will do all in his power to prevent the recurrence of such outrages and to punish the perpetrators . . . The king hopes that mutual goodwill and confidence will exist . . . In order to afford better protection, both to natives and to British subjects who may proceed there for purposes of trade, the King has sent the bearer of this letter, James Busby Esquire, to reside among you as H.M's Resident, whose duties will be to investigate all complaints."

The text was then read in Maori by Revd. Henry Williams who also urged the chiefs to protect Busby and to help him make his office effectual. In his own speech Busby expressed the hope that, when his house was built, the chiefs would visit him and be his friends: ". . . We will then consult by what means you can make your country and people a rich and wise people like the people of Britain . . . learn that it is the will of God that you should all love one another then wars will cease and your country flourish."

On an occasion marked by formality and the utterance of high-minded sentiments it was not lost on Maori that the King had not provided his Resident with any means of enforcing his authority. Such was the climate of suspicion which surrounded Busby's arrival that a rumour circulated among Maori to the effect that Busby, in conjunction with the missionaries, would receive payment for each Maori converted and that the final aim of his appointment was their eventual enslavement.

Following the reading of the King's letter a minor diplomatic embarrassment occured. The missionaries informed Busby that forty chiefs required presents to mark their attendance at his arrival. Busby, acting partly on instructions from the missionaries Hall and Yate whom he had met in Sydney, had brought clothing for only fifteen chiefs. The two missionaries had also provided him with a list of chiefs who in their opinion might be relied upon for help and who consequently should receive more generous presents than others. Not surprisingly the missionaries' list emphasised the names of Rewa, Titore, Te Morenga, Atua Haere, Patuone, Ripi, Hera and Hautungia, all of whom had signed Yate's letter to King William IV. With some gratitude Busby accepted the offer of blankets from the Mission's store and was thereby rescued from embarrassment on his first day as British Resident.

A NEW SETTLEMENT AT WAITANGI

It was to the missionaries that Busby turned for assistance and hospitality in the first few weeks of his appointment. More than any other European group they had influence over at least a section of Maori. At first Busby thought of settling at the mission and asked for a small piece of land near Paihia. According to Ramsden it was the missionaries who then directed his attention to the Waitangi headland nearby.

In May 1833 the land at Waitangi was controlled by two branches of the Ngapuhi Ngati Rahiri sub-group, the Ngati Kawa and Matarahurahu. Te Kemara was the principal chief of Ngati Kawa; Marupo and Hepetehi were the chiefs of Matarahurahu.

It will be recalled that the earliest purchase by Europeans of land at Waitangi had been made by the missionaries Kendall and Hall when in 1815 they envisaged it as an alternative site to the mission at Rangihoua. This purchase for five axes had been made with the old chief Waraki. Marsden's second attempt to establish a mission at Waitangi in 1823 was frustrated by the absence of chiefs with whom he could negotiate a land sale. During the intervening years Hall had retained ownership of the original land and it was he who had sold his deed of purchase to Busby when he met him in Sydney in 1826. The amount Busby paid him for the deed is not known.

Although Hall had advised Busby that he should make a further "accompensation" for the land to its Maori landowners, Busby did no such thing. Whether or not Busby intended to deceive the original landowners is difficult to know. That he had bought Hall's original deed was never revealed to the Maori chiefs or to the government of New South Wales. His own description of the "sale" before the Court of Land Claims at Russell, formerly Kororareka, on 28 January 1841 glosses over the facts:

" The Governor fixed my residence at the Bay of Islands and instructed me to consult the wishes of opinions of the Chiefs as to the most desirable situation for my residence—a meeting of the Chiefs of the northern part of the Island was called as far as they could be brought together and on 17th May 1833 they assembled at Paihia and they agreed among themselves that Waitangi would be the most desirable place—Before the materials had been moved from Paihia where they had been landed it was agreed that the land should be sold to me and the natives themselves moved over the materials and carried them up the Hill—I did not at that time understand the native language and I believe that a general assent of the parties interested that the land should be mine was given."

Barbara Fill describes Busby's account as subterfuge, and she points out that the missionaries knew of Busby's failure to disclose his purchase of Hall's deed: ". . . Between the time that he arrived at the Bay on 5 May 1833 and his official welcome which took place on 17 May, Busby, with Williams, had visited Waitangi and presented to the assembled chiefs as a fait accompli, his decision to reside there."

She continues: "It is not surprising therefore that due to Busby's ignorance of tribal movements in the area and the Maori attitude to landownership, he suffered the same fate as the previous European tenants at Waitangi—Hall, Conroy and Campbell and Dr Ross. It was only after the abortive attack on the Residency in April 1834, led by one of the owners of the land, Rete, that Busby heeded Hall's earlier advice and negotiated the purchase of the land on which his house was erected. His purchase of 270 acres at Waitangi in June 1834 was the first of his speculative land ventures at the Bay of Islands."

From these events it is difficult to avoid the conclusion that the missionaries and the British Resident himself, despite their believing themselves to be honourable bearers of superior values, were quite prepared to deceive the natives. At this early stage Busby may indeed have been ignorant of Maori communal landownership but the missionaries, on whom he relied for advice, certainly were not.

BUILDING THE RESIDENCY AT WAITANGI

In June the materials sent from Sydney on board the *New Zealander* were moved from Paihia to Waitangi by eight canoes. Work on building the house began the following month and payments were made in all to seven carpenters, six labourers, and a plasterer, all of whom were Europeans. Maori from Te Waimate supplied three thousand kauri shingles and seven thousand laths. An unspecified number of Maori labourers were paid for their work. As well as the Sydney prefabricated house an outbuilding was erected behind and this functioned as kitchen, storeroom and servants' room. Timber for it was supplied by Clendon and Stephenson, merchants of Okiato, near Russell.

Although Mrs Busby had arrived at Paihia in August, she and Busby continued to stay in Henry Williams' study and did not move into the Residency until 27 January 1834 at which stage their house still remained unfinished. From July work proceeded very slowly because extra tools and materials to replace wrongly supplied items had to be imported from Sydney.

The construction of the house began with the laying of large basalt boulders collected from the surrounding area. This was followed by the digging of a trench for the vertical framing posts and the careful erection of the framing whose studs were fixed to the top and bottom plates by mortise and tenon joints. For extra security these were pegged with hexagonal wooden pegs. The studs and plates of the framing were all marked with Roman numerals cut into the wood: thus a stud marked XVIII would be matched up to a plate marked XVIII and the two pieces mortised and tenoned together.

Joinery, door frames and architraves were of cedar and the interior of the house plastered, though it is no longer certain if the plaster was ever painted. Bricks for the two chimneys in the middle of the two main rooms at the back of the house and of the chimney in the kitchen-servants' quarter block were made in Parramatta, Sydney. Bricks were also used to line the walls of the house to a height of approximately six feet after which the supply of bricks was probably insufficient to continue.

The Roman numerals which allowed the builders of the pre-fabricated Residency to match up the timbers are still clearly visible.

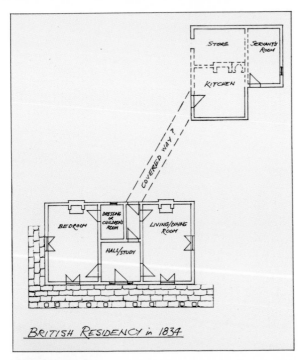

BRITISH RESIDENCY in 1834

The original Sydney-designed British Residency as it appears today.

The Sydney sandstone paving for the verandah and other surrounds had been shipped from "the Colony," the popular name for Sydney in the Bay of Islands, in large blocks. There was some difficulty in unloading such weighty stone from the canoes because in 1933 a number of blocks were discovered to be visible at low tide on the beach at Waitangi. They had lain there for one hundred years but the 1933 restorers decided to have them hauled up to the Treaty House so they might finally be put to their intended use.

Although by September 1833 the brick chimneys were being built there were problems when Cooper, Busby's servant, disappeared taking items from the store. On September 21 Henry Williams, no doubt eager to re-occupy the study he had cleared out at his "utmost inconvenience," confided in his journal, "Mr Busby in much trouble; his workmen leaving and the natives stealing their property; the prospect of a long residence with us." Some sign that construction was nearing completion was evident by December 23 when Williams sent five boys from the mission to help with the plasterwork.

The house, built according to the amended plan by Ambrose Hallen, consisted of two main rooms with a central hall divided probably to allow for a small dressing room. Unlike Verge's original the two main rooms were of equal size and at the side of each was a window instead of French casements which were a later addition. The classically derived turned verandah posts were not equally spaced as they have been since 1933 when the house was remodelled.

Nearby were Maori settlements. The largest, known as Taumata Mohi, was situated on the Paihia side of the mouth of the Waitangi River. There was another on the other side of the river on the beach where the Waitangi wharf is today. It is possible that this was also the location of the "wretched hut" described by the French explorer and scholar Dumont d'Urville, who visited the Busbys in 1840. Possibly it could have been the dwelling occupied by the two convict sawyers, Conroy and Campbell during Hall's brief 1816 residence at Waitangi. According to Ngapuhi oral tradition there was another settlement behind the Residency to the north west of the house but all evidence of it has now disappeared. Isolated individuals also occupied whare on Busby's property.

THE ATTACK ON THE RESIDENCY

On 30 April 1834 just sixteen hours after the birth of John, the Busby's first child, the Residency was attacked. Mrs Marianne Williams, wife of Henry, and a surgeon from a whaler anchored in the Bay had been present at the birth. Mrs Williams had only just left when she was called back to comfort Agnes who was greatly agitated though still largely ignorant as to exactly what had happened.

At the time of the attack Agnes was in bed with her new baby in one of the two larger rooms; the other was occupied by three workmen employed to continue building the still unfinished house. James Busby, exhausted from the long vigil at his wife's bedside, was sleeping in the hall. When he was awoken by his servant, William Moore, Busby opened the front door, walked out on to the verandah and looked around the side of the house to see what was happening at the store behind the house. Two shots were fired at him. He rushed to the back door to call the female servant in from the kitchen but on putting his head out the door was fired on again, receiving cuts to his face from a shaft of splintered wood caused when a bullet hit the doorpost. Workmen came to his aid and scared off the attackers but not before they had managed to plunder Moore, the servant's, bedroom. Busby later recorded that within half an hour the commanders of all the vessels in the Bay had arrived at the Residency accompanied by armed men. Next morning came chiefs shocked at the nature of the attack on the King's representative whose person they had declared tapu. The attitude of the some of the European settlers, already sceptical of the worth of a Resident with no visible means of authority, was decidedly less sympathetic.

What actually precipitated the attack remains unclear. There is a distinct possibility that it was an act of utu in response to Busby's occupation of the land at Waitangi without first purchasing it from its Maori owners. On the other hand, it is possible that the attackers were more interested in the small supply of arms which was kept in Busby's store.

Whatever the motivation the search for culprits went on for weeks. The settlers were keen to use the opportunity to see how effective Busby could be in the role of Resident; he was put under much pressure to insist upon redress and a petition to the British Government seeking armed protection was circulated. Busby himself felt insulted by such independent action taken before he had a chance to decide how to deal with the situation.

Then Henry Williams organised a meeting of thirty nine chiefs to try to identify those responsible for the attack. All were adamant that the offenders should be apprehended and punished. Shortly afterwards the prominent Ngapuhi chief Hone Heke, who had been educated at the Mission School at Kerikeri and

The hall, complete with Busby's bed, is furnished as it would have been on the night of the attack on the Residency.

39

was a close friend of Williams, arrived at the Residency. He carried a rug which Busby at once recognised as having been stolen from Moore's room on the night of the attack. It had been found in the possession of Rete, one of the original landowners of Waitangi. As a result it was he who was charged with leading the attack. Under pressure from the assembled chiefs Rete confessed and was forced to agree to the confiscation of some of his land at Puketona and a period of exile. Busby believed he should be put to death for an action which he regarded as an offence not against himself but against King William IV.

Powerless, Busby several times put his situation before Governor Bourke who did not reply probably because he knew only too well that to accede to Busby's requests would involve the New South Wales government in expense it certainly wished to avoid. Busby was anxious in the first place to have the Residency guarded and although Governor Bourke did grant him sixty pounds to employ twenty Maori for this purpose he refused Busby's request for old uniforms in which to dress his guard.

Rete's land at Puketona was confiscated though he was never exiled. The following year Busby was infuriated to hear that Rete had actually built a number of new whare on what the chief still obviously regarded as his land and was regularly walking close to the Residency. Busby complained that the chiefs had failed him in not enforcing Rete's exile. In retaliation he burned Rete's whares, an action which caused great resentment to the point where the missionaries warned Busby that he himself might well suffer retaliatory action. Earlier Busby had agreed that the former Maori landowners could keep their whare on the land at Waitangi for use when they were fishing but he now considered that those associated with Rete had forfeited this "privilege."

In retrospect, the 1834 attack on the Residency at Waitangi served to highlight many deficiencies in the terms of Busby's appointment. The settlers, already sceptical, were only confirmed in their doubts. Some like the merchant Samuel Polack took to criticising openly Busby's understanding of Maori language, custom and habits and his apparent foolishness, even arrogance, in choosing a promontory so distant from traders, Maori and missionaries as the site for his home. The fact that the New South Wales government had ensured that Busby was acting in a vacuum without its assistance or blessing was now clear. For his part Busby responded to the situation by becoming extremely sensitive to slights against his position and even came to believe that the missionaries, particularly Henry Williams, who should have been his closest allies were usurping of his authority as Resident. Feelings of distrust and antagonism now existed between Maori and the British Resident to such an extent that Busby a year after the attack thought it "worse than useless" to call a meeting of the chiefs.

But Busby certainly now realised the importance of paying formally for the two hundred and seventy acres he occupied. On 30 June 1834 he and Henry Williams met with the Maori landowners of Waitangi led by Hone Heke, a relative of Rete with whom he shared the title at Puketona. This was the first of three meetings at the conclusion of which one hundred and ninety seven pounds sixteen shillings and a variety of goods at Sydney prices were paid for the land. Not surprisingly at this stage Busby's relationship with the Maori improved.

That he eventually came to understand the necessity for sensitivity in dealing with Maori is also evident from his response to a situation which arose shortly after he had completed the purchase of the land at Waitangi. When the chief and **tohunga** Tohetapu died, his body was placed in a box daubed with red ochre and raised on poles above the ground where it was to lie for a year until his **hahunga** or death feast. The tomb was to be situated close to the Residency so Busby consulted Henry Williams to see if it could possibly be moved further away. The Busby family history records that: ". . . after a tremendous amount of negotiation and utu paid to the chief's relatives, and they seemed legion, the body was removed to some other quiet spot . . . for all the time he was at Waitangi he was obliged to pay utu for the **wahi tapu**." The site of the tomb, probably beneath the present Waitangi Hotel, was thereafter designated tapu.

LIFE AT WAITANGI

Despite the small size of the new Residency it frequently became a temporary home for visitors. As the wife of the British Resident Mrs Agnes Busby was often called on to be the hostess at dinners and on important political occasions to supervise catering arrangements for very much larger groups. On such occasions she had the older daughters of missionaries for assistance and there was usually some form of domestic help though it was not until after 1840 that a married couple, appropriately named Mr and Mrs Tidy, remained in the Busby's employ for a substantial length of time.

Between the years 1834-1843 the Busbys had six children: John, Sarah, James, George, William and Agnes. James died in Sydney in April 1840, Agnes of whooping cough at Waitangi in 1847 and George as the result of a shooting accident at Waitangi in 1847. James Busby was competent domestically but was often away so Agnes Busby's life could hardly have been easy. Their eldest daughter Sarah was expected to help around the house as soon as she was old enough and when the Revd. William Cotton stayed at the Residency on 26 March 1844 he left a touching record of the couple's domestic existence: ". . . Sarah Busby acting as nursemaid, sweeping the room—she does capitally entering into

The British Residency.

Waitangi (now Haruru) Falls.

all that is to be done, taking care of the baby—as though she understood it all. The youngest child, a girl about a year old had been cross all night with teeth, had broken Mrs Busby's rest or rather prevented her from having any and she had a bad headache this morning. Mr B. acted both as cook and nurse of the baby feeding it before our breakfast began. He remarked whilst it was very cross "The more trouble these little things are for us, the more we love them, much more than when we had servants to do all this."

One of the first visitors to the Residency as it was originally built was Edward Markham grandson of the Archbishop of York and a young traveller who later published his recollections of New Zealand. He arrived at Waitangi on 20 July 1834, a Sunday. After attending church at Paihia he and the Busbys returned home where they ate a dinner of pork, potatoes and bread and drank a bottle of port. Following an afternoon nap he and Busby walked over the Resident's recently purchased estate. Markham left a frank impression of his hosts, "Mrs B. is very pleasant, he is rather too formal and Religious for me to be quite at ease with, but he was particular kind and helpful." The following month Markham returned to Waitangi for some days and there witnessed the trial of Rete for his attack on the Residency.

A more eminent visitor was the great botanist Charles Darwin who arrived in the Bay of Islands on board the *Beagle* under Captain Robert Fitzroy in December 1835. Although Darwin certainly visited Busby at Waitangi, he left no detailed account of what took place at the house merely recording that Busby took him on a journey up the river to see the "pretty waterfall" and also helped to organise a guide who would convey Darwin safely to Waimate. On Christmas Day he attended Divine Service at Paihia where he commented on the tediousness of bi-lingual prayers and the inferiority of the natives' singing to that heard in Tahiti. It is perhaps surprising to the modern reader that such a well educated scientist should so blatantly exhibit characteristics of cultural superiority evident in his descriptions of Maori dwellings, the traditional Maori facial tattoo or **moko** and the greeting by pressing noses together known as the **hongi**.

He quotes with evident approval "a pleasing anecdote" told to him by Busby, which, Darwin writes, is a proof of the sincerity of at least some of those Maori who profess Christianity:

". . . one of [Busby's] young men left him, who had been accustomed to read prayers to the rest of the servants. Some weeks afterwards, happening to pass late in the evening by an outhouse, he saw and heard one of his men reading with difficulty by the light of the fire, the Bible to the rest; after this the party knelt and prayed; in their prayers they mentioned Mr Busby and his family and the Missionaries, each separately in his respective districts. Mr Busby then went in and told them how glad he was to see how they were employed; they replied they had done so ever since the first young man had gone and so should continue."

Darwin reserved his most positive comments for the admirably English appearance of the mission at Waimate; he did not like New Zealand and was glad to leave it.

Waterfall at Waitangi River—from Manners and Customs of the New Zealanders Vol.2.
Joel Samuel Polack. (1840)
ALEXANDER TURNBULL LIBRARY

BUSBY THE HORTICULTURALIST

One of the few vistors to comment on the appearance of Waitangi in these early years was J.B. Williams of Salem, Massachusetts, the American Consul in New Zealand. He visited Busby, whom he described as a "worthy and urbane gent." In his journal for the years 1842-44 he wrote of Waitangi:

"A more delightful and romantic spot it would be difficult to find in the Bay . . . Mr Busby has displayed great taste about those parts of the grounds he improves, doubtless Mrs Busby must share in the credit as his worthy spouse . . . I well remember the first call I made at their pretty, neat and hospitable Mansion embodied in a grove of trees and shrubs, with flowers sending forth a rich fragrance. Mr Busby has quite a large farm under cultivation, and a fine grapery propagating fast."

Indeed Busby was a considerable horticulturalist. In 1823 he had visited vineyards at Capetown on his voyage to Australia with his emigrating family and later wrote a manual of Plain Directions for Planting and Cultivating Vineyards and for Making Wine in New South Wales. In 1831, while awaiting news of a possible Colonial Office appointment, he toured a number of French and Spanish vineyards and in 1833 and 1834 published two accounts of his visits. During the tour he collected thousands of cuttings which were packed in moss and shipped back to New South Wales. They were planted at his sister and brother-in-law's property at Kirkton in the Hunter Valley, and at the Sydney Botanical Gardens.

One of Busby's first acts on arriving at Waitangi had been to establish a nursery for his vine cuttings and other plant seedlings. Most probably some of these cuttings would have been collected during his tour of Spanish and French vineyards. In 1836 Busby planted a vineyard at Waitangi, the exact location of which is uncertain though his grandaughter maintained that it was sited between the house and the flagstaff and was later destroyed by soldiers who camped there.

In 1840 the commander of the *Astrolabe,* Dumont D'Urville, sampled some of the wine produced at Waitangi. It was, he wrote, "a light white wine, very sparkling and delicious to taste which I enjoyed very much. Judging from this sample, I have no doubt that vines will be grown extensively all over the sand hills of these islands and very soon New Zealand wine may be exported to English possessions in India!" Alas, the sheep and cattle which Busby brought from Sydney in 1840 wreaked havoc with his vineyard. Inadequate fencing brought an early end to a promising experiment.

Busby was intensely interested in horticulture and the garden at Waitangi was filled with exotic and native plants. Returning from his 1831 trip to England he not only brought vines but seeds of tomatoes, watermelon, pimento, cucumbers, lettuce, currants, sultanas and other vegetables. The kitchen garden

The cabbage trees which Busby planted as a windbreak to protect his cultivations.

at the Residency kept the household supplied with fresh vegetables, Revd.Cotton mentioning that on his visit in September 1842 he had been given fresh asparagus to eat. Records of deliveries from the Sydney Botanical Gardens show that during 1842 Busby received peach, olive, apple and loquat plants.

Some of Busby's trees survive today, most spectacularly the large Norfolk pine—lone survivor of a row of such trees planted by Busby but felled in 1845 by Maori. Cabbage trees, still a prominent feature of the gardens, were apparently planted by Busby to shield his vines from easterly winds. The gardens at Waitangi were at their height during the years 1838-44 but damage done by the army and by Maori raiding parties during Busby's absence in 1845 and 1846 meant that they never maintained their early glory.

Neither was Busby any more successful in his attempts to establish a productive farm at Waitangi. In this he was largely thwarted by a shortage of labour but he did plant some crops near the house. In 1839 he bought the area known as Puke to the north west of Waitangi intending to carry out a cattle breeding enterprise. Storms, labour difficulties and financial problems precluded the success of this precarious operation.

Ever an optimist Busby in a letter dated 9 April 1839 mentions his intention to convert part of his Waitangi estate into residential town sections. This was to be the town of Victoria, Busby's preferred designation for Waitangi and certainly his most grandiose scheme. It was to have been situated to the immediate south and west of the Residency and was to include a pier, marketplace, parks, gardens and streets bearing such names as Wellington and Peel. As late as 1846, six years after he had first drawn up the plan, Busby was still placing advertisements for sections in the newspaper The New Zealander though few were ever sold. Like the vineyard and the cattle breeding farm, the town of Victoria remained an unfulfilled dream.

Busby's last remaining Norfolk pine is still a prominent Waitangi landmark.

The arrangement of cabbage trees in rows indicates the site of Busby's vineyard.

(Left) The site of Busby's planned township of Victoria.

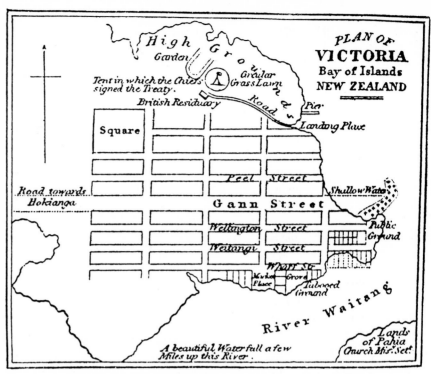

The following labels appear on the map:

PLAN OF VICTORIA Bay of Islands NEW ZEALAND

High Ground / Garden / Circular Grass Lawn / Roads / Tent in which the Chiefs signed the Treaty. / British Residency / Pier / Landing Place / Square / Peel Street / Shallow Water / Road towards Hokianga / Gann Street / Wellington Street / Public Ground / Waitangi Street / Wharf St. / Market Place / Grove / Tabooed Ground / River Waitangi / A beautiful Waterfall a few Miles up this River. / Lands of Pahia Church Mis. Sett.

The 1840 Wyld plan of the layout of Busby's Victoria includes some unusual spelling.

THE RESIDENT AS POLITICIAN

When Busby first arrived in 1833 to take up his position as British Resident the town of Kororareka was firmly established as the commercial centre of the Bay of Islands. Its economic success depended on its function as a port where visiting shipping could be serviced. Markham described the town as having enough grog shops to accommodate up to three hundred men from thirty whaling ships anchored in the Bay . . . and their ladies. To the missionaries the town seemed a hotbed of licentious behaviour though they recognised that many of the traders who operated successful businesses there were respectable people who wished to live in a respectable society. Although Busby had the title of British Resident they quickly realised that he could be of little use to them or guarantee the kind of society they wanted.

When the Residency was attacked by Maori, Busby appeared unable to deal effectively with the apprehension of culprits. A group of traders wrote a letter demanding that he "bring the natives of this country to a proper sense of the treatment to be observed to the representative of the British Government in a foreign country." But Busby had no authority for direct action and, as Lee points out, "his only weapon was diplomacy, which he used in the ensuing years with varying success."

Busby's time was taken up with disputes among the Maori and European community though occasionally he was asked by the New South Wales Government to assist in apprehending convicts or deserters from ships. Settlers who called upon him in an attempt to get something done usually felt frustrated at his inability to help them in any way. As a result they invariably took matters into their own hands and set up their own institutions for the maintenance of law and order.

In September 1833 the Kororareka Union Benefit Society was formed to introduce regulations preventing the sale and consumption of liquor when missionaries were present. This piece of window dressing was designed to improve the image of the town in the eyes of respectable folk. There was also to be a prohibition on gambling on Sundays. Busby was consulted and missionaries at Paihia were invited to preach at Kororareka. But there was nothing Busby could do of a practical nature to enforce these regulations even had he wished to.

Kororareka Beach 1828. Lithograph.
Sketches illustrative of the native inhabitants of New Zealand, London 1838.
Augustus Earle (1793-1838)
ALEXANDER TURNBULL LIBRARY

In 1838 a group of traders took the law into their own hands and actually utilised the cruel punitive technique of tarring and feathering someone accused of larceny. The hapless victim was dumped into the sea and although Busby expressed his disapproval of such harsh measures he could not provide an alternative to the traders using their own methods, however inhumane.

Somewhat incongruously in view of his activities as a winemaker Busby was the president of New Zealand's first temperance society. On 11 May 1836 he took the chair at the inaugural meeting of the Kororareka Temperance Society, giving an address which was was later published by the Church Missionary Society's press at Paihia. Apparently the society only called this one meeting; it was ridiculous to contemplate enforcing restraints on alcoholic consumption particularly in a town where sailors came ashore specifically to enjoy themselves after the deprivations of long and frequently unpleasant sea voyages.

Ships at Anchor, Kororareka 1840.
Louis Le Breton (1818-1866)
Hand-coloured lithograph
AUCKLAND CITY ART GALLERY
This idyllic scene belies the description of Kororareka as a hell hole of the Pacific.

How little improvement was effected at Kororareka can be judged from the comments of the surveyor Felton Matthew who arrived in the Bay on 29 January 1840:

"Of all the vile holes I ever visited this is certainly the vilest. It consists of some twenty cottages (some tolerably good ones) exclusive of native huts, standing on a shingly bank of some very small extent . . . of the town it is impossible to speak in terms which can convey an adequate idea of my disgust— the half-drunken, devil-may-care sort of look of the European inhabitants, and the squalid debased appearance of the natives form a tout ensemble which has certainly produced anything but a pleasing impression on me."

Among Busby's routine duties was that of customs officer. He kept shipping records of whalers because all whale oil coming into British ports was subject to customs duties unless it had been documented as having been obtained by British crews. Thus Busby was able to certify that the American ship *Erie,* which had a British crew, could pass through Customs without paying any duty. It was during the period of his Residency that American whaling activity expanded greatly. In 1839 sixty two American whalers were recorded as having entered the Bay by the merchant and acting American Consul, James Clendon.

NEW ZEALAND'S FIRST FLAG

Early in his period as Resident it appeared as though Busby would be able to use his position as registrar of shipping and his Sydney-bequeathed function as utiliser of chiefly authority for the maintenance of order between Maori and settlers. He had become aware of a problem arising from the fact that ships built at the Horeke shipyard on the Hokianga Harbour had no official national flag under which to sail. Vessels were liable to be seized in foreign ports and vulnerable to acts of piracy. In 1830 the cargo of one such vessel, the *Sir George Murray,* had been seized at Sydney, an action which caused grave offence to the chiefs Patuone and Te Taonui who were on board at the time.

Three flags— whether designed by Busby or Revd. Henry Williams is not certain today—were made up in Sydney. They arrived in March 1834 on board *HMS Alligator* and on the 20th, Busby, thirty chiefs and Captain Lambert with his officers from the *Alligator* assembled at the British Residency to chose the first flag of New Zealand. An oblong tent had been put up on the lawn in front of the Residency; inside the flags were displayed on short poles. The votes of assembled chiefs of the Bay of Islands and Hokianga were recorded: twelve for the first, ten for the second and six for the third; two of the chiefs abstained. The winning flag—dominated by the Red Cross of St George on a white ground—

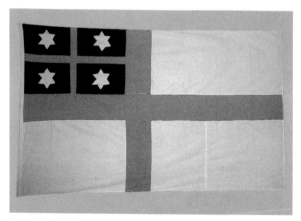

New Zealand's first flag.
MAORI WOMEN'S WELFARE LEAGUE

49

was hoisted with the Union Jack as a twenty one-gun salute was fired from *HMS Alligator.*

Claudia Orange has pointed out that Busby went to some pains to make the flag selection an impressive event. In associating chiefly mana with that of a national flag he no doubt hoped to achieve some kind of a public relations coup but his diplomatic skills were not equal to the task. He failed to allow the chiefs the opportunity to debate their choice so those who abstained did so because of their fear of some sinister intent. Worse still, he excluded some chiefs from the voting because he considered them of inferior rank and at the celebration feast which followed he even served the Maori chiefs separately from the Europeans. Finally, his insistence that chiefs carrying weapons be disarmed whilst officers of the *Alligator* wore ceremonial swords was extremely tactless. The hope that the flag conference might lead to a Confederation of Chiefs came to nothing and Busby's intentions remained unfulfilled.

In December the British Admiralty approved the new flag as the national flag of New Zealand. It was flown at Waitangi and Captain Fitzroy observed it flying elsewhere in the Bay when he arrived on the *Beagle* in 1835.

THE DE THIERRY INTERLUDE

On 9 December 1835 an American brig, *Charles Doggett,* arrived in the Bay with a letter from Papeete, Tahiti written by a French baron who informed Busby and the missionaries he had "declared the sovereign independence of New Zealand—that is my own independence as Sovereign Chief" and that he was coming "with armed ships, with guns, and with property." This gentleman signed himself Charles, Baron de Thierry, Sovereign Chief of New Zealand and King of Nukuhiva. Busby was convinced that the letter was the work of a madman and even Governor Bourke in Sydney noted in the margin of a copy of the letter hastily forwarded, "this looks like insanity."

Baron Charles Philip Hippolytus de Thierry was born in 1793. His aristocratic family fled to England to escape the French Revolutionary violence. In 1820, while de Thierry was a student at Cambridge, he happened to meet the missionary Thomas Kendall who had travelled to England with the chiefs Hongi Hika and Waikato. So impressed was he with the two chiefs that he then and there became "carried away with an ardent desire to benefit [the New Zealanders] and to establish a colony there." De Thierry gave Kendall nearly eight hundred pounds to purchase 40,000 acres of land. In 1822 when he returned to New Zealand, Kendall obtained the signatures of the chiefs Muriwai, Patuone and Tamati Waka Nene on a deed of purchase for land on the north eastern shores of the Hokianga River. The chiefs were paid thirty six axes, Kendall having already spent the Baron's money elsewhere.

On receiving the deed of purchase from Kendall, de Thierry had it sent to the Secretary of State for the Colonies in London who smartly informed him that his request for a loan of eight thousand pounds with the deed as security in order to start his proposed colony was refused. De Thierry then left England in 1826 to pursue other grandiose schemes in the United States, the West Indies, the Marquesas Islands and Tahiti; while he was in Panama the Congress of Bagota actually granted him for a fifty year period all rights to the cutting of a Panama Canal.

In his letter to Busby de Thierry declared that he wished to make known his intentions and to discover from the Resident what kind of reception he might expect "either as New Zealand's best friend or her enemy!" In the copy sent to Governor Bourke Busby meaningfully underlined this phrase. The Baron had outlined in the document a scheme of government that included parliamentary representation for Maori and proposed that both races should live as equals in a society unencumbered by taxes.

Although it was apparent that de Thierry was a creator of "hopelessly visionary plans" as Judith Binney calls them, some kind of definite response was necessary to counter his long-nurtured schemes, particularly as they seemed to embody a vague military threat. Busby wrote to Governor Bourke that "there appeared to be sufficient method in the madness of such a man, to be productive of much mischief, and that it became my duty to give anxious consideration to the most effectual means of frustrating such an attempt as he had formally announced."

By the end of 1835 Busby had become convinced that the political situation in the Bay was so volatile that the smallest spark would kindle the flame of war. Maori who supported the missionaries' activities were vigorously opposed by others, led by the chief Waikato, who did not. There was a distinct possibility that the military energies of rival Maori factions could be utilised. Busby also knew that it would still be possible for someone like de Thierry, a non-British subject, to purchase huge pieces of Maori land very cheaply. Alarmed at the prospect of war, Busby tried but failed to get Governor Bourke to send military aid so that a French invasion could be repelled.

Busby's first action was to have the missionaries print an address to the settlers which exhorted them to inspire Maori with a spirit of resistance to anyone who might attempt to usurp sovereignty over them. He next informed de Thierry that he could expect to be fiercely resisted if he tried to put his threat into action. Messengers were despatched with copies of the following message

Baron Charles de Thierry (1793-1846)
AUCKLAND MUSEUM

translated into Maori:

"O friend; Hear ye—a letter has been received from a person affar who desires to be King of the Maori poeple. I think that you should all meet at my house . . . that I may hear your opinions of this interfering person, and as to what shall be done. Shall the land be handed over to him, and all you be slaves or not?

Busby, Resident of King William."

A DECLARATION OF INDEPENDENCE

On 28 October 1835 thirty four chiefs assembled at Waitangi, among them Waikato, no friend of Busby's, vigorously denying that he had ever invited de Thierry to govern New Zealand. Tamati Waka Nene, who was absent on the occasion, had declared that the axes with which Kendall believed he had purchased land for de Thierry were never regarded by Maori as the price of the land. The chiefs decided unanimously to have nothing to do with the Baron's schemes. Busby then produced his Declaration of Independence. This document, he explained with the aid of the missionaries, was designed to get the chiefs to act in concert and declare the independence of their country, asserting their exclusive rights to its sovereignty.

The chiefs, as the United Tribes of New Zealand, agreed to meet annually at Waitangi though it was not to be until February 1840, on the occasion of the signing of the Treaty of Waitangi, that they were actually all brought together again. The chiefs also sent a copy of the Declaration to King William IV asking him to be their protector.

Busby thought the United Tribes of New Zealand was the best guarantee against a takeover by foreign powers and to this end he continued to collect signatures to the Declaration. Copies continued to be circulated but inter-tribal enmities proved stronger than any hope of concerted action. Timber obtained by Busby for the building of a Parliament House was never used.

In the end Baron de Thierry too was unable to carry out his scheme. In financial difficulty he remained at Papeete buying coconut oil to pay for his passage to Sydney, eventually arriving at Hokianga on 4 November 1837. There he offered the Europeans already living on his territory three acres free of any lease for every one in cultivation—provided that they recognise him as "Lord of the Soil." With him came sixty emigrants but no army.

Barbara Fill has, perhaps extravagantly, described de Thierry as a shattered visionary. In the following years he lived in poverty constantly harassed by both Maori and Pakeha on a piece of land at Waihou, the property of Tamati Waka

Nene. In March 1844 he was awarded fifteen hundred acres on the Waihou River and another piece of land at Pakirikiri was given him by the chief Te Taonui. These he later exchanged in order to buy land at Auckland where he moved to in 1845. He spent some years on Pitcairn Island and in San Francisco, returning to Auckland in 1853 where until his death in 1864 he made a living by teaching music and processing flax.

TOWARDS THE TREATY

By the late 1830s the Resident's powerlessness to act decisively in all but minor disputes helped to create an impression of disorder in the Bay of Islands. Busby's own dispatches, invariably containing requests for help, only heightened this impression in Sydney and in London. Although in the aftermath of the Declaration of Independence Busby was derided because of what was interpreted as his over-reaction to de Thierry's threatened action, the Declaration and his Residency in general did have a significant effect upon Maori, as Claudia Orange has pointed out. It prepared them to accept further British intervention in their country.

They had become increasingly concerned about sales of their land to Europeans, particularly in the period 1837 to 1840 when land speculation flourished. Now thwarted in Australia by legislation, it was enthusiastically pursued here by those who wished to take advantage of Maori ignorant of the true value of their land and prepared to sell it for European manufactured goods of relatively little value. Loss of land always meant loss of mana to Maori, thus resentment grew.

The activity of land sharks exacerbated Maori fears. Such activity was not finally put a stop to until as late as 19 January 1840 by which time much of the Bay of Islands had already been sold. A Sydney auction due to sell two thousand acres of Bay of Islands land was only prevented when Governor Gipps, Bourke's successor, issued a proclamation declaring future purchases of land in New Zealand made by British subjects null and void. But there was no way to prevent speculators selling at great profit land they had already bought very cheaply from the Maori.

Naturally, law abiding settlers' anxiety increased about what might happen if Maori resentment should ever become actively directed against them in a concerted way. As Lee pointed out, settlers tended to believe that Maori were incapable of governing themselves. They also knew that in 1835 Busby had, with the Declaration of Independence, nominally guaranteed the chiefs sovereignty. Settlers had no formally constituted political rights whatever. For some the threat of foreign intervention must have seemed an ever-present possibility, despite the ludicrousness of de Thierry's attempt.

In 1837 the settlers' worst fears about the possibility of Maori disruption seemed about to come true. An act of cannibalism led to a serious outbreak of inter-tribal fighting in the Bay of Islands and a petition was sent to King William IV. It described lawlessness which Busby was powerless to prevent and it asked for protection. The Resident requested a warship or some kind of armed force for this very purpose but as Claudia Orange has written, "the heart of the matter was that the petitioners wanted more than the half-hearted official commitment represented by Busby."

Although outbreak of inter-tribal war was eventually prevented without European intervention, Governor Bourke reluctantly decided to order *HMS Rattlesnake,* under the command of Captain William Hobson, to the Bay of Islands. Now even Busby should have been satisfied. From 26 May 1837 Hobson spent just under one month interviewing traders, missionaries, chiefs and settlers and on his return to Sydney advocated the establishment of specific sites or factories to be areas of British jurisdiction after securing the agreement of the chiefs. What both Hobson and the Colonial Office seemed to have in mind was a solution Britain had already used in North America and was shortly to use in Shanghai. Busby wanted to go further. He wrote a report proposing the establishment of a British Protectorate with the Crown administering local affairs in trust for all inhabitants, with the assistance of chiefs. Busby's and Hobson's reports arrived at the Colonial Office in London in late 1837 and early 1838, long after the events which had precipitated them had passed. They were nonetheless influential in changing the climate of opinion in favour of some direct British action in New Zealand. This was mainly because of pressure from the New Zealand Company and a softening of previous hostility to the idea of colonisation.

As the result of these changes the tide of opinion swung inexorably in favour of the colonisation of New Zealand. The solution adopted by the British Government was most unusual. In February 1839 it appointed Captain William Hobson to the post of Consul. This decision had been hastened by news that in May the New Zealand Company's ship *Tory* had sailed from England to make the first land purchases for the company. Even then New Zealand did not become a sovereign state. Instead the boundaries of the colony of New South Wales were now extended to include New Zealand.

Lieutenant-Governor William Hobson of New Zealand (1839)
Mary-Anne Musgrave (nee Heaphy) active 1821-1847
REX NAN KIVELL COLLECTION,
NATIONAL LIBRARY OF AUSTRALIA

FROM RESIDENT TO LIEUTENANT GOVERNOR

On 29 January 1840 Captain Hobson arrived with a rather more impressive entourage than Busby could muster. Most importantly he was accompanied by a force of mounted police and a magistrate. Their ship, *H.M.S. Herald* was commanded by Captain Joseph Nias under whose instructions the twenty-gunned frigate slowly drifted with the tide until it dropped anchor off Kororareka. At the Residency across the bay at Waitangi the Union Jack was flying though those on board were more intrigued to see the French tricolore fluttering on a hillside above Kororareka.

On shore there was initially some confusion as to the identity of the *Herald* because she failed to hoist a pennant. A row brewing between Captains Hobson and Nias had erupted during the ship's wind-less journey down the bay after Nias, already put out at being expected to pay deference to a brother officer, refused to raise a pennant until he had reached an anchorage. Hobson had demanded that he do so much earlier in order to indicate to James Busby that the Resident should be prepared to come on board immediately.

Eventually Busby, the missionary Charles Baker and the mission printer Colenso boarded the *Herald*, hastily explaining that the French flag indicated the location of a Roman Catholic Church and the residence of Bishop Pompallier. Hobson took Busby to his cabin where he gave him the letter which announced the termination of his appointment as British Resident, something Busby could hardly have been surprised about. They then set about drafting a letter in Maori inviting the chiefs to meet the Governor at Mr Busby's residence at Waitangi on the following Wednesday, February 5th. An announcement to all British residents was also prepared requesting their presence at the Mission Church, Kororareka on 30 January, the following day, to hear the proposal for the extension of the colony of New South Wales and the appointment of Hobson.

Colenso worked into the night to have the Maori notices in circulation the next morning. The letter to the chief Tamati Waka Nene has survived and read:

Of the thirtieth day of January 1840.

My Dear Friend,

Here again is mine to you. It is that a ship of war has now arrived with a Chief on board, who is from the Queen of England, to be Governor for us. Now, he desires that there shall be assembled together all the Chiefs of the Confederation of New Zealand on Wednesday of next holy week, so that they may meet him. I therefore say unto you, friend, that you come here to Waitangi, to my home here, to this gathering. For you yourself are a Chief of that Confederation. That is all, mine ends.

From me, your dear friend, BUSBY.

Admiral Sir Joseph Nias
AUCKLAND MUSEUM

Not until next day at two o'clock precisely the scrupulously proper Hobson landed on shore at Kororareka. He was wearing his full naval dress uniform gleaming with gold lace. His arrival was accompanied by the roar of the *Herald's* guns although Nias, continuing what the Sydney Herald later described as a "tiff," refused to grant Hobson the thirteen-gun salute of a Lieutenant Governor and fired only the eleven deemed appropriate for one with the rank of Consul.

In fact there is some reason to believe that Hobson was exceeding his instructions in assuming the Lieutenant Governor-ship at this point. Lord Normanby at the Colonial Office in London had originally intended that Hobson should land in New Zealand as British Consul, negotiate a treaty with the chiefs which would result in their ceding their sovereignty to the British Crown and only on completion of this process proclaim himself Governor of the territory formerly under the jurisdiction of the treaty's signatories.

Hobson's decision to assume the role of Lieutenant Governor before negotiation did not meet with Busby's approval either. Extraordinary though it may seem, Hobson knew about Rete's attack on the Residency at Waitangi in April 1834. He knew too that Busby had chosen not to take the attack personally, regarding it instead as an attack on the person of King William IV and as a result had demanded the confiscation of Rete's land at Puketona. Now, nearly eight years later, Hobson wished, *as Lieutenant Governor*, to read his proclamation of the extension of the colony of New South Wales to New Zealand on the very piece of land which he believed to have already been conveyed to the British Crown's representative. In the right for once, Busby told Hobson that he was mistaken. The land at Puketona had never been ceded by the natives and Hobson was therefore premature in adopting Governorship before these important legalities had been attended to. From a practical point of view he also shrewdly pointed out that Puketona was wholly inaccessible.

Despite these objections both Busby and Nias accompanied Hobson to the church at Kororareka though, as Buick points out, it was fortunate that they were the only people to take exception to Hobson's actions on constitutional grounds. There would undoubtedly have been those who listened to Hobson's proclamation with something less than enthusiasm since it signalled the end of land purchasing from the Maori. It is said that there were those among would-be land buyers who attempted in the few remaining days to whip up Maori opinion against the cession of sovereignty by putting it about that the result would be the virtual enslavement of the entire people. The proclamation also signalled the inevitable introduction of an official system for the maintenance of law and order in place of the arbitrary and frequently cruel justice dispensed by the Kororareka Association. In general Hobson was well received, forty five of the settlers presenting him with an Address of Welcome expressing their pleasure at the prospect of British law and authority in the Bay.

PREPARATIONS FOR A TREATY

The first days of February 1840 were spent in the necessarily hasty preparation of the treaty document, the terms of which needed to be formulated with the greatest care. Hobson, who was now ill, retired to his cabin and devoted himself to the writing of a document which outlined the Crown's obligations and the benefits Maori would receive. His rough notes were then sent across to Waitangi so that Busby could submit his views. Busby later wrote "the draft of the Treaty prepared by me was adopted by Hobson without any other alteration than a transposition of certain sentences, which did not in any degree affect the sense."

Revd. Henry Williams, head of the Church Missionary Society in New Zealand, was not present when Hobson first arrived at Kororareka, having been absent in Manawatu. He received a note from Hobson on the morning of 30 January at Waimate and by the afternoon was on board the *Herald* where he professed the support of the missionaries in establishing a Crown authority.

On the afternoon of Tuesday 4 February Hobson brought Williams a draft of the treaty which he proposed to submit to the chiefs on the following day at Waitangi. Williams and his son Edward, a fluent Maori speaker, had the task of translating the treaty document into Maori. Busby and Henry Williams laboured long into the night over the wording, Busby eventually giving his personal assent to the document. Revd. Richard Taylor was on hand to copy the words.

On the lawn in front of the former Residency, now the private home of Mr and Mrs James Busby, the sailors of the *Herald* were busy erecting a marquee made from the framework of the ship's spars and a covering of sails. It was surrounded by a number of smaller tents intended to shelter Maori whose rank might preclude them from a place in the larger marquee. According to Dr Bright of Adelaide, an eyewitness to the events, the sloping ground was "neatly planted with native and exotic shrubs which shaded a verdant turf." On the river bank where the Te Tii Marae now stands Maori were camped in readiness for the event to follow; canoes plied the Bay though the picture painted by Buick is probably more fanciful than accurate:

"their crews keeping time with their paddles to the chant of the excited **Kai-tuki** as he stood upon the centre thwart, urging by word, song and gesture, a more vigorous bending of the broad brown backs and straining of tawny arms in the hope of outstripping their opponents in the race to Waitangi."

Revd. Henry Williams (1792-1867)
AUCKLAND MUSEUM

WEDNESDAY 5 FEBRUARY 1840

At one end of the marquee a raised platform had been built on which seats and a Union Jack-draped table had been placed. The sides of the tent were decorated with a selection of the *Herald's* flags. The Union Jack fluttered from the flagstaff until the official proceedings began, whereupon it was lowered to signify that the cession of sovereignty had not yet taken place. According to Dr Bright, a gentleman who wielded a fanciful pen, food and drink were freely available to Maori and European before the official party arrived. Observing that armed Maori greatly outnumbered Europeans he described his reaction: "What, thought I, if these savages refuse to accede to the treaty, is to hinder them from driving us into the sea, or into their ovens?"

At nine o'clock Captain Hobson accompanied by Captain Nias landed at Waitangi and walked up to the former Residency. Inside the house James Busby, Revd. Henry Williams and Revd. Richard Taylor were still busily discussing the translation of the document. At 10.30 in a blaze of purple and gold the Roman Catholic Bishop of Oceania, Bishop Pompallier, accompanied by a priest, walked without hesitation into Busby's house, entering the room where the other

The Landing of Captain William Hobson from HMS Herald, Waitangi, Bay of Islands, 5 February 1840 for the signing of the Treaty of Waitangi.
Matthew Thomas Clayton (1831-1922)
Oil on canvas (1896)
AUCKLAND CITY ART GALLERY

The bay at Waitangi where Hobson landed now bears his name while the track up to the former Residency, now the Treaty House, is named for Captain Nias. The captain of the *Herald* is also commemorated by the stone seat situated half way up the track.

gentlemen were conferring. The two constables on guard at the door were so taken by surprise that they did not even challenge the Bishop's right to enter. Maori, observing this spectacle as the Bishop knew they would, did not fail to register the arrival of such an obviously important figure.

Neither did the Anglican missionaries who had been standing deferentially outside. Now, after a hurried conference, they moved towards the house. As they did so Hobson announced that all those who wished to meet him could enter through the front door and, having greeted him in the passage, could leave by means of one of the French casements. But as Bishop Pompallier remained at Hobson's side during the introductions there was insufficient room to allow the missionaries to stand with them. They chose to remain outside.

The introductions over, James Busby, preceded by four Sydney policemen, walked out of the house followed by Captains Hobson and Nias, walking arm in arm, obviously having patched up their earlier differences. Before they had gone very far Bishop Pompallier and his priest quickly stepped forward ahead of the CMS missionaries who had once again to follow. A distressed Revd. Richard Taylor wrote that: "the Romish priest keeping so close behind the Governor that, though I tried hard, I could not get between." The dignitaries were then seated

Bishop Pompallier (1801-1871)
AUCKLAND MUSEUM

and the missionaries loyally took up position behind Revd. Williams on the dias. The main aisle was reserved for the more aristocratic chiefs, Europeans arranging themselves on either side. From the clear space in front Maori speakers would address the assembly.

Now Hobson, relying on copious notes, spoke first, emphatically and with strong feeling according to the surveyor Mr Felton Mathew. He told the chiefs that their assent was essential to the establishment of British law. He assured them that Queen Victoria was as ready to protect all her subjects as she was to restrain them. He guaranteed them time to consider the proposed treaty which was, he affirmed, expressly drawn up for their own good. He reminded them that it was they who had often asked her predecessor, King William IV, for his protection and that here at last was a treaty offering such protection. Hobson then read the treaty in English. When he had finished reading he turned to Revd. Williams and asked him to read the translation of the treaty in Maori.

When Williams completed the reading he invited the chiefs to express their views or to ask for further clarification of its points. In the period of hesitation which followed Busby stood up and delivered a speech assuring them that the treaty did not mean that they would lose their lands but, more importantly, would guarantee their continued possession of land not already sold. As he was in full flight, justifying his own practice of not recognising ownership of improperly purchased land, the Ngati Kawa chief and tohunga Te Kemera, former owner of the coastal land at Waitangi, sprang up:

"O Governor, my land is gone, gone, all gone. The inheritances of my ancestors, fathers, relatives, all gone, stolen, gone with the missionaries. Yes they have it all, all, all. That man there, the Busby, and that man there, the Williams, they have my land. The land on which we are standing this day is mine ... I say go back, go back, Governor, we do not want thee here in this country."

It must have been an awkward moment for Busby who had bungled his original purchase. But worse was to follow. Te Kemera was followed by Rewa of Ngaie-Tawake. Although his opening English greeting "How do you do, Mr Governor?" caused a burst of laughter, he soon spoke as forcefully as Te Kemera, with the same emphasis that the Governor should return to his own country. Moka of the Patukeha hapu of Rawhiti agreed. When his words were interpreted to Hobson, the Governor rose to assure everyone that all land purchases made before his proclamation would be the subject of inquiry and any unlawful purchases returned. Moka, scarcely reassured, immediately turned on the Revd. Taylor demanding return of his lands. Baker apparently replied enigmatically "We shall see whether they will return."

Now the settlers, who up to this time had been silent, began to complain that the missionaries were not translating accurately what was being said by either Maori or English speakers. This, from a Kororareka dealer in spirits, brought from Williams the reply that the first land purchases to be inquired into should be the missionaries' for they would be found entirely in order. Next, Busby, possibly nervous lest his own dubious dealing be revealed, averred saying that "I never bought any land but what the natives pressed me to buy, for which I always paid them liberally."

Now it was the turn of Tamati Pukututu who made a speech flatly contradicting the sentiments of his predecessors; he was followed in the same vein by Matiu. They were the to first speak in favour of the treaty. The chief Tareha advocated an equality of rank between the Governor and the chiefs; another, Whai, asked pertinently of Hobson if he thought that the white man, who had not listened to Busby, would be any more likely to listen to a Governor. The battle waged for four hours between those who wished Hobson to stay and those who insisted on his leaving, emphasis falling heavily in favour of those who wished him to leave the country forever.

Hone Heke (? - 1850)
AUCKLAND MUSEUM

One of the most forceful speakers was the missionary-educated chief Hone Heke. Here was a high ranking Ngapuhi chief directly descended from Rahiri who would be listened to with great attention. According to Colenso's eye witness account Heke said "This, my friends, is a good thing. It is even as the word of God." He stated that if Hobson left, Maori, whom he described as children, would fall to the mercy of rum sellers and the French. "Remain I say, Governor, remain. A father, a Governor for us." Other accounts say that Heke spoke violently and contradictorily but certainly he was followed by other chiefs in favour of the treaty and the Governor's remaining.

Tamati Waka Nene, whom Bright described as a "mild-looking, middle-aged man with a deportment as if he felt he was a gentleman," had listened to Heke with a smile on his face. In Nene's view it was too late for Maori to try to remove the Europeans; he argued that the Governor would protect his people, that his presence would ensure peace and that Maori would not be doomed to enslavement if they agreed to the treaty. His speech was crucial in swaying the opinion of the gathering. Nene was followed by his brother Patuone who spoke in a similar vein. These conciliatory speeches from Heke, Nene and Patuone were too much for Te Kemera who reiterated his original opinion vehemently. In reply Busby tactlessly announced that Governor Hobson would be occupying his house at Waitangi until a suitable residence could be built for him. Te Kemera's patience was exhausted. He advanced towards Hobson holding his hands together as though handcuffed, demanding "Shall I be thus?" Reproached for his insolence by other chiefs he now ran forward grabbing Hobson's hands shaking them and shouting "How do you do, Governor." Tension was thus released by

Tamati Waka Nene (? - 1871)
AUCKLAND MUSEUM

Patuone (? - 1872)
AUCKLAND MUSEUM

laughter and amid cheering and applause the meeting was adjourned until Friday 7th to allow Maori further time for discussion.

THURSDAY 6 FEBRUARY 1840—THE SIGNING OF THE TREATY OF WAITANGI

After a night of prolonged discussion among themselves the chiefs decided that the debate about the treaty should be concluded one way or the other as soon as possible. Food was running short and many of those who had come long distances were anxious to set off on their return journeys. Despite the earlier decision to meet on the Friday Maori gathered in tribal groups on Busby's lawn by mid-morning. There they waited.

None of those on board the *Herald* had any idea what was afoot, Hobson having in fact sent some further alterations to the wording of the treaty suggested by Busby to Revd. Taylor so that he could have the document re-copied ready for the meeting planned for Friday 7th. When a boat from the *Herald* made its leisurely way across the bay its occupants were surprised to hear on landing that many people were waiting for His Excellency on the lawn in front of the former Residency. A message was sent to Hobson who came ashore so quickly that he did not have time to change out of civilian clothes. He and his party walked at once to Busby's house whilst Maori moved into the tent. A table for the signing was hastily set in place and the Governor and his party ascended the platform.

Hobson announced that there would be no discussion as to the merits of the proposed treaty but that he was willing to accept the signatures of any chiefs prepared to sign the document.

Before signing began there was an interruption when Hobson received a message that Bishop Pompallier and his priest had arrived at Busby's house and were anxious to attend the meeting. The Bishop was invited to enter the tent and took the same seat he had occupied at the table the previous day. This time his purpose was to ensure that the colonisation of New Zealand should respect free toleration in matters of faith and he asked that a public guarantee of this should forthwith be made in Maori. Revd. Williams, though outraged, quickly drafted a statement which not only satisfied the Bishop, who left immediately, but also specifically acknowledged the protection which the Governor likewise guaranteed Maori custom. The missionary rather deviously hoped that the association of the Roman Catholic faith with what Busby called "heathen practices" would be detrimental to both. There was one further interruption. Colenso the printer had become increasingly alarmed at the speed with which events were moving and was convinced that some of the chiefs did not understand the nature of the treaty which now lay before them. Some had arrived late, after the discussions of the previous day had concluded. As Busby was about to begin calling out the names of each chief so that he could come forward to sign, Colenso asked Hobson whether he was satisfied that the chiefs understood what they were signing. There was a brief interchange during which the Governor stated rather naively that if there was any misunderstanding it was no fault of his. Now Hone Heke, whose name had already been called, wrote his name in English at the top of the first column of the parchment then turned to the chiefs expressing his approval of what he had just done.

He was followed unhesitatingly by others despite noisy speeches from the chiefs Marupo and Ruhe who ran up and down, stamping their feet and gesticulating, the former to the point of exhaustion. When Marupo realised that his words were having no effect he, like Te Kemera the day before, went up to the Governor, shook his hands violently and placed his braided hat upon his own head. Marupo then signed the treaty with a design from his moko. He was followed by Te Kemera and then by Rewa who volunteered the information that it was the French Bishop who had initially enjoined them not to sign. As each chief signed Hobson shook him by the hand saying **He iwi tahi tatou—We are now one people.**

When all the chiefs had signed Patuone came forward to the dias to present Hobson with a greenstone **mere** intended as a gift for Queen Victoria. He was then invited to dine that evening on board the *Herald* where, in Felton Mathew's condescending words, "he used the silver with perfect grace and ease, took wine with everyone at table, ate moderately, and was perfectly self possessed as if accustomed to the best English society from his infancy." Other chiefs were each presented with a gift of two blankets and some tobacco.

On the following day, Friday 7 February, which Hobson had originally intended as the day of signing, the weather was so stormy that no one could leave the *Herald*. Next day was fine again; the ship ran up all her flags and a 21-gun salute was fired in celebration of Britain's new colony.

In the months that followed signatures of chiefs were gathered at meetings held throughout New Zealand. By September 1840 five hundred signatures had been collected, though chiefs of the Te Arawa and Tuwharetoa tribes refused to sign. Others, like those who objected at Waitangi, did so with considerable reluctance, demanding that Maori should govern themselves and not cede their **kawanatanga**. Today it seems clear that few Maori understood exactly what they were ceding to the British crown or perhaps what was involved in signing such a document. In addition there was confusion of meaning in translating some of the treaty's crucial terms from English into Maori.

Wellington artist L.C. Mitchell made this colourful painting of the treaty signing in 1948. It is closely based upon Buick's description of the events of 6 February 1840. Hobson shakes Hone Heke's hand as Marupo and Ruhe exhibit disapproval of his action.

There were without doubt chiefs who were attracted by the thought that the treaty would result in increased opportunities for trade. It was widely believed too that the Governor's future involvement in land sales would protect Maori from the unscrupulous activities of speculators. Claudia Orange has given emphasis to the fact that many Maori relied on the advice of the missionaries when formulating their own attitudes to the treaty. Revd. Henry Williams presented the treaty to Maori as a sacred covenant between them and the Queen of England as head both of the church and the state. If the treaty did indeed have such spiritual as well as temporal force then there would be few who could resist it.

JAMES BUSBY AND THE FORMER RESIDENCY AFTER THE TREATY

With the arrival of Hobson, Busby's official service was concluded; henceforth he was to live with his family as a private citizen on his land at Waitangi. Busby may have thought that he could find a position under his successor and indeed in later life maintained that he had been offered a post in Hobson's administration but had declined it. True to his word the Governor proclaimed that all land purchased before 1840 would now be subject to investigation and that claimants with large holdings would be limited to 2,560 acres. In the years which followed Busby's time was to be much taken up with litigation concerning his personal land claims.

Full of ambition to succeed in business now that his period as British Resident was over Busby entered into a sawmilling partnership with Gilbert Mair and William Lewington at Ngunguru. Their purchase of some 40,000 acres was actually made soon after Busby first heard the news of the termination of his official appointment and on a date some three weeks after the date on which all private purchases from Maori were to have stopped. Possibly Busby did not take Hobson seriously but after the proclamation it appeared that his Ngunguru land purchase would also be subject to investigation.

In April 1840 Busby and his family left New Zealand for the first time since his arrival in 1833. In Sydney, where he had gone to seek prospective markets for his timber, he protested his right to the land he had purchased after having learned to his dismay that Governor Gipps was sponsoring a bill which went even further than the proclamation and proposed cancelling all existing land titles in New Zealand prior to February 1840. For motives which were transparently self serving Busby addressed the Legislative Council in New South Wales on 30 June 1840, speaking in vehement opposition to the bill and thus occasioning Governor Gipps' lasting enmity. Though Gipps did admit that Busby's position as ex-Resident might entitle him to special consideration the matter remained unresolved for many years.

On 24 October 1840 Busby chartered the barque *Thomas Laurie* and the following month returned with his son John to the Bay of Islands with a cargo of cattle and sheep. Building materials were also sent for the purpose of erecting houses and a store on the land at Victoria and for the express purpose of enlarging the former Residency.

The tiny house had long needed more rooms in order to accommodate not only the growing number of children but also those visitors who stayed sometimes for a number of nights rather than just for a meal. Busby had been planning extensions as early as 1838. Now there were delays in beginning the work because the carpenter Busby brought from Sydney rejected some of the timber supplied locally by his partner Mair. It was possibly not until 1841 that the scantling and boards, laths and shingles brought from Sydney were used to build a skillion or lean-to on to the back of the house. This probably housed three rooms; a bedroom, a dressing room and a pantry, and an extension of the passage to a new back door. The small dressing room originally at the back of the original house would have lost its window and thus have become very dark.

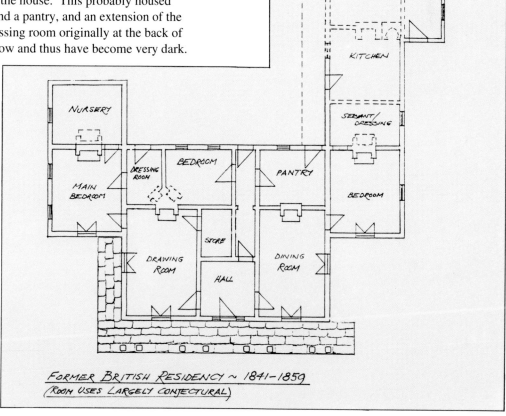

FORMER BRITISH RESIDENCY ~ 1841-1859
(ROOM USES LARGELY CONJECTURAL)

Although there have been suggestions that the two wings were added to the back of the house at this time, it is more likely that they were built as late as 1846 or 1847, though a portion of both wings may well date from 1841-42. The side windows of the original house were converted, probably to French casements, at the same time as the wings were added. The north wing now connected the original 1833 house to the kitchen/storeroom area, adding a bedroom and what might well have been a servants' dressing room. The south wing was provided with a new bedroom (where the exhibition room is now) and a nursery beyond.

Even as he began extending his house Busby received another blow. In the previous seven years he had gradually acquired eight different pieces of land adjoining his property at Waitangi. Now it appeared that his tenure of these 1000 acres was shaky and that the greater part of his Waitangi land holding would be reserved for a township. Hone Heke and others chiefs supported Busby's claim to the land even when it was revealed that he had sold small portions of it for larger sums than he had paid for it. It was not until 1844 that his possession of the land at Waitangi was finally confirmed by Governor FitzRoy, Hobson's successor.

But meanwhile worse financial problems emerged. The sawmilling partnership had failed to raise enough money to pay shipping charges. By mid 1841 Busby needed to raise more money and travelled back to Sydney where he was reunited with his family on 9 June 1841. None of Busby's efforts to secure capital in Sydney was a success and the whole family returned to Waitangi in November. The next two years were spent trying to establish a profitable farm and travelling back and forth between the Bay and Sydney in attempts to find a market for timber milled at Ngunguru. By November 1843 it was quite apparent that none of Busby's entrepreneurial schemes was going to succeed and in 1844, on the brink of financial ruin, he was forced to sell his stock. In June 1844 with a bank threatening to seize his property Busby in desperation boarded an American whaler returning to the United States, taking with him thirty tons of kauri gum for sale. Fortunately this particular transaction was profitable and he was able to clear his debts. He returned home via England in March 1846.

THE NORTHERN WAR

The Bay of Islands was in turmoil during Busby's absence in the United States and in England. The removal of the capital of the new colony from Kororareka to Auckland in 1841 had a serious effect on the Bay. The introduction of customs levies in the period of rationalisation following the signing of the treaty forced prices up; now shipping levies were paid directly to the government rather than to private individuals. Land sales all but ceased as the result of the carrying out of Article 2 of the Treaty.

Despite the fact that the Ngati Rahiri chief Hone Heke had signed the treaty he became the focus of discontent among those Maori who blamed the economic depression on the destructive influence of pakeha. More moderate Ngapuhi leaders like Tamati Waka Nene opposed Heke's increasingly aggressive attitude, particularly his chopping down of the flagstaff bearing the British flag at Kororareka on July 8, 1844. Such was the atmosphere of menace in the town that by February 1845 a military presence had become necessary at Kororareka where disturbances of the peace now fuelled pakeha resentment. By March 1845 Heke was determined to put an end to British authority in the Bay and assembled a large force just south of Kororareka. On 11 March, after he had cut down the flagpole for a fourth time, fierce fighting broke out; the town was evacuated then bombarded by *HMS Hazard.* Afterwards it was looted and occupied by invading Maori until 17th. The alarmed inhabitants of Kororareka moved to Auckland in large numbers.

At the end of April 1845 a punitive force from the 58th and 96th Regiments, newly arrived from Sydney under the command of Colonel William Hulme, assembled at Kororareka. There followed a military engagement between Maori and European forces at Heke's Te Kahika pa at Okaihau. Then his Te Ahuahu pa near Lake Omapere was captured by Te Taonui, an ally of Nene's. Heke's new pa at Ohaeawai survived a heavy three-week bombardment but was razed to the ground when on July 11 1845 it was captured but found to be abandoned. Heke and his people had already escaped unscathed. After Heke himself was wounded in a later skirmish he continued a paper war, sending Governor Grey, who had replaced FitzRoy, a letter which the Governor found offensive:

"God made this country for us. It cannot be sliced; if it were a whale it might be sliced. Do you return to your own country, which was made by God for you. God made this land for us; it is not for any stranger or foreign nation to meddle with this sacred country."

The war ended in January 1846 after the two week-long bombardment of Ruapekapeka pa in which the British force was assisted by Nene, Patuone and other chiefs. Neither Kawiti, Heke's powerful ally, nor Heke himself was captured. He and his followers were granted a free pardon by decree of Sir George Grey on 24 January 1846.

This war had severe implications for James Busby and his family as they were quickly to discover on returning home in March 1846. The Bay of Islands was no longer a prosperous trading centre, all business now being centred on the new capital at Auckland. Their house at Waitangi had been left empty in March

1845 when Mrs Busby and the children had fled to Sydney to escape the violence. Maori war parties ransacked its interior and stripped lead from the roof but fortunately Revd. Williams had taken the precaution of removing all doors and windows, storing them at Paihia. In January 1846, with Busby's permission, army officers took over the now dilapidated former Residency, their commander Major Cyprian Bridge occupying three rooms and his fellow officers eight others. The officers do not appear to have left the house until July so conditions for the family after their arrival in March would have been most trying. In addition to his pressing financial problems it can only have been deeply depressing for James Busby to observe the ruined condition of his formerly magnificent gardens after they had been ravaged first by Maori plunderers and then by European troops who camped on the lawn or were quartered at nearby Victoria.

Waitangi from Busby's Victoria 1864
John Kinder (1819-1903)
AUCKLAND CITY ART GALLERY

The artist has depicted a pastoral scene near Hall's Gully looking back towards the Te Tii lowland.

(Left) **Paihia, Bay of Islands** 1864
John Kinder
AUCKLAND CITY ART GALLERY

During the next twenty five years Busby was involved in almost continuous disputes over his land claims at Ngunguru, Waipu and Whangarei. He was never again employed officially except for a brief period as a justice of the peace but from 1853, when he took his seat in the first Auckland Provincial Council, was well known as the leader of those claimants who had bought land before Hobson's proclamation. Ramsden, in discussing Busby's role as a Provincial Councillor comments that, "there were times when he elicited sympathy in the Council, when he even secured generous acknowledgment that wrongs remained to be righted. There were times, too, when his persistent, often monotonous advocacy angered colleagues. Home truths relating to past events were resented."

Between 1861 and 1863 Busby was editor of a newspaper, the Aucklander, which had been established to promote the views of the old land claimants, as they were popularly known. Persistent to the last, Busby travelled to England again in 1865 but was refused a hearing by the Colonial Office. Finally in 1868 he received thirty six thousand eight hundred pounds in compensation for his lost land. He had already spent fourteen thousand in legal costs.

In the years Busby was involved with politics, land claims and newspaper work his two sons, John and William managed the farm at Waitangi. Other than minor repairs little work was done on the house because Busby simply did not have the money to spend on such things. In 1859 he ordered shingles from Waimate for roof repairs; in 1868 some of the window sashes were renewed.

Kororareka, Bay of Islands 1858
John Kinder
AUCKLAND CITY ART GALLERY

Rangihoua, Bay of Islands 1864
John Kinder
AUCKLAND CITY ART GALLERY

The Revd. John Kinder visited the Bay of Islands in December 1858 and January 1864, taking photographs, sketching and later making characteristically picturesque watercolours of places associated with missionary activity. As an Anglican clergyman Rangihoua was important to him as the site where Marsden preached his first sermon on Christmas Day 1814.

On 15 July 1871 Busby, who had returned to England for an eye operation, died at Penge, Surrey of congestion of the lungs. Agnes Busby, his wife, returned to Waitangi and continued to live at the former Residency with her son John and his wife. There she occupied a suuny bedroom in the north wing. In front of Mrs Agnes Busby's bedroom was a conservatory with French doors opening into the drawing room on the right side of the hall. In 1882 when the house and land were sold Mrs Busby went to live with her daughter Sarah, married to William, son of Revd. Henry Williams. Agnes Busby died at Pakaraka on 12 October 1889.

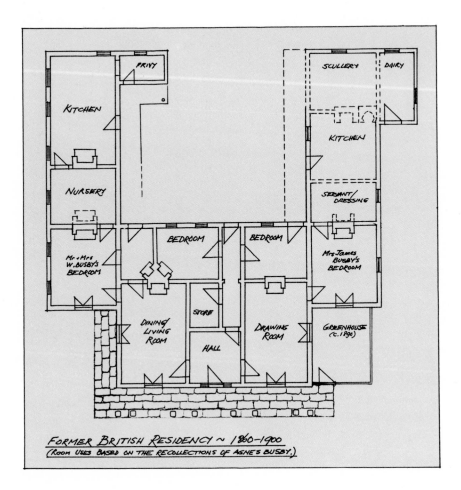

FORMER BRITISH RESIDENCY ~ 1860–1900
(ROOM USES BASED ON THE RECOLLECTIONS OF AGNES BUSBY.)

FACING PAGE:

Waitangi photographed c. 1870 by D.L. Mundy
ALEXANDER TURNBULL LIBRARY

The site is now open farmland and at the extreme left a timber windbreak shields what remains of Busby's orchard.

The former British Residency photographed c. 1882.
ALEXANDER TURNBULL LIBRARY

The glasshouse tacked on to the front of the house is clearly visible. Busby's gardens have disappeared.

Where the Treaty of Waitangi was signed. 1882.
Alfred Sharpe (c.1830-c.1912)
AUCKLAND CITY ART GALLERY

The painter had himself rowed out to the islands in the harbour in order to capture this picturesque view of an historic spot.

Where the treaty of Waitangi was signed.

The former Residency, in great disrepair, was photographed by Russell Duncan in 1903 before its new owners began their renovations.
ALEXANDER TURNBULL LIBRARY

The former British Residency in 1905. Work has now begun on restoring the house. Busby's Norfolk Pine is already prominent.
GODBER COLLECTION, ALEXANDER TURNBULL LIBRARY

THE FORMER BRITISH RESIDENCY 1882-1932

When the Busbys finally left Waitangi in 1882 the house and land were sold to John Hyde Harris, a farmer who over the next twenty years took out a number of mortgages on the property. Photographs taken during the period record a house in sad decline. In 1885 the former Residency was occupied by William King, grandson of the CMS missionary John King who had arrived with Marsden at Rangihoua in 1814. He and his wife Eleanor managed the property and it is likely it was they who were responsible for its being given a corrugated iron roof. During the 1890s the house appears not to have been lived in at all; verandah posts broke away from the structure they formerly supported, the conservatory and floor levels collapsed and shutters hung awry. Apparently the two front rooms were used as a shearing shed.

On 21 September 1900 Harris's land was put up for auction at a mortgagee sale at which James Busby's sons John and William were the highest bidders. The land was conveyed to them by the Registrar of the Supreme Court. It is believed that it was William Busby's intention to dismantle the now derelict house and to built a shack for a caretaker of the property. Fortunately for posterity this plan changed.

In December 1900 a Wanganui sheep farmer Eustace Gordon Hewin who had decided to move to the Bay of Islands met William Busby at Paihia and inspected the Waitangi property. On 17 December 1900 he bought the derelict house and surrounding land. For five years he did very little with the house but in 1905, following his engagement to Clarissa Williams, decided to renovate it.

Many years later his wife recalled her first impressions of the former British Residency which was now to be her home. "Sheep had been camping in the house, its roof and ceiling were falling down, sacks replaced glass in the windows and altogether the house was very dilapidated. Actually it would have been more economical to pull the place down and rebuild, but sentiment prevented my husband from taking this step."

Between 1901-03 Mr Hewin carried out extensive renovations to make the house habitable. Internal plaster walls and ceilings were replaced with timber lining, scrim and paper; foundations were repaired and kauri joists used to replace rotten floor boards. The remnants of the glasshouse on the north side were finally removed and the entire north wing demolished. The north facing side walls of the main house and skillion now became a continuous outside wall. A new verandah was built on eight equally spaced square posts with ornamental fretwork above. Exterior architraves, doors, corner boxing and the verandah posts were picked out in dark paint and the few remaining shutters removed altogether. Thus the original Sydney facade lost the colonial Georgian appearance which John Verge had given it in 1833, now taking on the appearance of a conventional Victorian villa. Sometime after 1912 a small low lean-to was added on to the north front but otherwise the house remained unchanged until 1933.

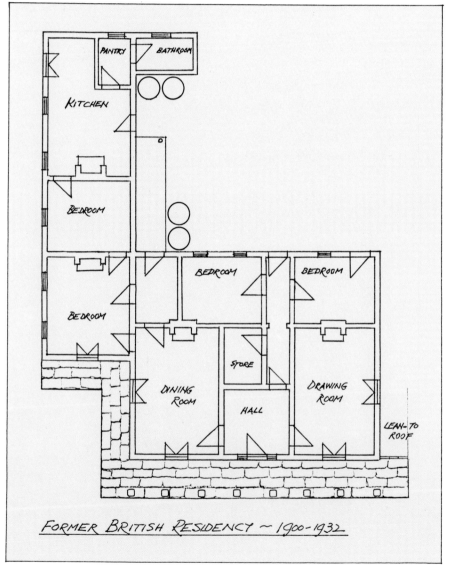

FORMER BRITISH RESIDENCY ~ 1900-1932

The former Residency photographed c. 1920-25 shows how a corrugated iron roof and a modified verandah treatment gave it the appearance of a Victorian villa. The shutters have disappeared.
ALEXANDER TURNBULL LIBRARY

"The spot where the Treaty of Waitangi was signed" 1905
RUSSELL DUNCAN ALBUM, ALEXANDER TURNBULL LIBRARY

THE BLEDISLOE GIFT

Sir Charles and Lady Elaine Bathurst, Lord and Lady Bledisloe - donors of Waitangi to the nation. This genial and intelligent man was known as "chattering Charlie" and his wife greatly admired for her friendly charm.
ALEXANDER TURNBULL LIBRARY

During the late 1920s the house began to deteriorate again and Mr and Mrs Hewin tried unsuccessfully to sell their Waitangi property. Their failure came to the attention of a local lawyer and M.P., Mr Vernon Reed. As the site of the former British Residency and the place where the Treaty of Waitangi was signed Reed, with considerable foresight, regarded it as a place of extraordinary historic importance and he tried several times to persuade the government to buy the land as a national monument. During the previous thirty years the insignificance of Waitangi merely reflected pakeha disinterest in the treaty itself. But New Zealanders knew that in 1940 the centenary of New Zealand was to be celebrated; preparation for a huge centennial exhibition in Wellington was already underway. Unsuccessful in his attempts to persuade the government to purchase the Waitangi property, Reed now approached the Governor-General Viscount Bledisloe of Lydney with the suggestion that Waitangi should become a national memorial.

Although today it may seem unusual that a dyed-in-the-wool English aristocrat should have become so personally involved with Waitangi, Lord Bledisloe's actions must be viewed within the context of other commemorative gestures planned for 1940. On 10 May 1932, following a visit to Waitangi, he informed the Prime Minister George Forbes by letter: "I desire formally, on behalf of Her Excellency and myself, to present, through you, to the nation, New Zealand's most historic spot"Waitangi" together with 1000 acres of land belonging to the estate of which it forms part and which we have recently purchased with this object."

In November a Deed of Trust set out the objectives for a National Reserve which included priority being given to the repair and restoration of the former Residency which, at Lord Bledisloe's request, was now re-named the Treaty House. On the Board of the Waitangi National Trust incorporated by Act of Parliament were the donors, Lord and Lady Bledisloe as life members; Mr Vernon Reed; the Prime Minister Mr Forbes; Alfred Ransom, Minister in charge of the Scenery Preservation Act; Sir Apirana Ngata, the Native Minister; Kenneth Williams, a member of the Williams missionary family, Riri Maihi Kawiti representing the families of Hone Heke, Maihi Kawiti, Tamati Waka Nene and Pomare; the Maori King, Te Rata Mahuta; Sir Robert Heaton Rhodes, representing the people of the South Island; Sir Francis Dillon Bell, representing the family of Edward Gibbon Wakefield, founder of the New Zealand Company, and Mr Gordon Coates, former Prime Minister of New Zealand.

It was decided to rebuild the north wing of the Treaty House as accommodation for a custodian and to transform the south wing as a display area. The objective was the restoration of the house as it was believed to have existed in 1840. Two of New Zealand's most eminent architects, W.H. Gummer of Auckland and W.M. Page of Wellington were commissioned as Honorary Architects.

On October 28 1932 Sir Apirana Ngata, speaking in the House of Representatives, drew members' attention to the fact that the centenary of the signing of the Treaty of Waitangi was but eight years off and that consequently a carved meeting house should be built at Waitangi by the Maori people, led appropriately by Ngapuhi, to commemorate the Governor-General's generous gift to the nation. The Whare runanga and the restored Treaty House were intended to be officially given to the people of New Zealand at the same time.

The vice-regal party during their visit to Waitangi in the summer of 1932. Lord Bledisloe favoured a heavy tweed suit in all weathers.
ALEXANDER TURNBULL LIBRARY

Mr Vernon Reed explains . . . the Bledisloe party in front of the former Residency, Summer 1932.
ALEXANDER TURNBULL LIBRARY

The rear exterior skillion wall of the former Residency photographed by Mr Norman Carless in 1932.
MISS MARGARET CARLESS.

The newly named Waitangi Treaty House in 1934 following restoration of the former Residency by W.H. Gummer and W.M. Page, honorary architects to the Waitangi Trust Board.
ALEXANDER TURNBULL LIBRARY

The rear of the house retains the appearance given it by Gummer.

THE 1933 RESTORATION OF THE WAITANGI TREATY HOUSE

Although Mr and Mrs Hewin were still living in the house the architects immediately began their preparatory work at the Treaty House so that it could be ready for an official opening on February 6 1934. Gummer appointed Mr Ralph McComb of Auckland as builder and, following a number of site visits, instructed him to begin work on the house in March 1933. There was a great deal of work to do as McComb reported in a detailed description of his work.

Floors had sunk, ground plates disappeared into the earth, the roof was leaking, doors and windows were ill-secured. The kitchen chimney was offset and half carried on the ceiling joists. So loose was the brickwork that it seemed a miracle to McComb that the entire house had not burned down.

First, the demolished north wing was completely rebuilt symmetrical with the south wing. The restoration of the main block of the house involved two separate areas; the original 1834 block and the skillion which had been added in 1841. In the main drawing room the original chimney was retained to ceiling height but rebuilt above; three other chimneys had to be demolished and two rebuilt in new brick. The front verandah was demolished then rebuilt on new kauri turned columns in equally spaced pairs. The original Sydney sandstone paving was lifted and relaid. Exterior weather-boards were replaced where necessary with pit-sawn kauri; a kauri shingled one displaced the corrugated iron roof; a new six-panelled front door replaced the four-panelled original; all French casements were replaced in kauri. At the rear the skillion was demolished and redesigned with narrower rooms to allow for a back verandah.

Inside, the kahikatea floors in the dining and drawing rooms were replaced after McComb discovered the extent of timber rot caused by water under the house. A new floor was laid in the hall using old boards: matchboard-lined scrim and paper walls were replaced with Tentest Insulating board covered with a coat of plaster. All cornice mouldings were replaced. The south wing, too, was all but demolished and a reinforced concrete "muniment" room built to house historic exhibits.

Although the restored structure was to become familiar as the "original" Treaty House, the Gummer/Page restoration produced a building which was seven eighths new. Many of the original materials including door leaves, sashes, sills, architraves and a pair of French casements had been re-used but the 1933 Treaty House was certainly a significantly modified version of Verge's original. Gummer's love of symmetry was apparent in his equal spacing of the verandah columns as was his fondness for accurate classical detailing in his providing them with plinth and abacus, unlike Verge's simple originals.

The restoration was finished by Christmas 1933 in time for the official opening on 6 February 1934. Before a huge crowd the Union Jack was unfurled at the top of the 90-foot flagstaff marking the site of the treaty signing; a series of Maori orators spoke; songs and haka were performed. Seated on a totara Coronation chair given by South Island Maori with a fine piece of tangiwai greenstone beneath it, Lord Bledisloe spoke of the "delight in the hearts of all those assembled in their thousands here today who join with me in regarding the co-operation and unanimous fealty of the Maori people to the British Crown and the British connection as a basic condition of national welfare and progress in this Dominion."

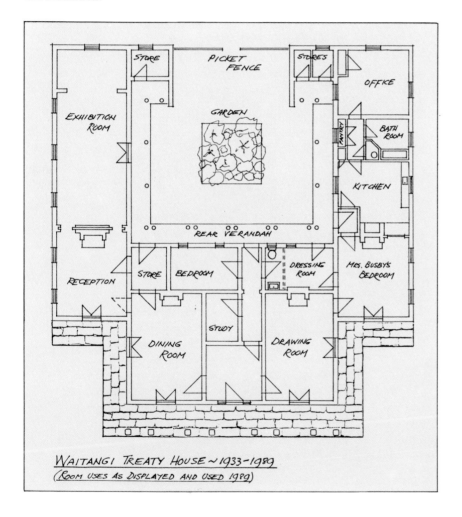

WAITANGI TREATY HOUSE ~ 1933-1989
(ROOM USES AS DISPLAYED AND USED 1989)

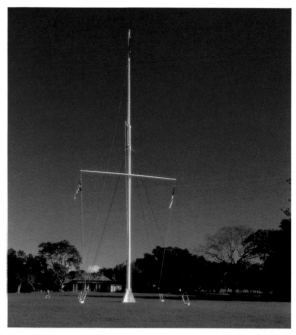

A flagstaff was erected in 1934 to mark the spot where the Treaty of Waitangi was signed in 1840.

The original chimneys were too unsteady to retain so Gummer designed new ones. The roof shingles were replaced with new kauri ones supplied by Mr Tau Henare.

In the late afternoon, praising the "abounding generosity of the Ngapuhi Tribe," he laid the foundation stone of the Whare runanga emphasising in his speech the importance of nurturing traditional Maori art and building practices.

Lord Bledisloe's intentions were evident when, with some pride, he looked out over the prospect at Waitangi at the restored British Residency, the flagstaff flying its emblem of British sovereignty and the site of the meeting house. He ventured to hope that this "triple association of significant structures on this hallowed spot be deemed, at this crisis in the history of the world, to typify the determination of our two races, whose joint heritage is this highly favoured Dominion, to cultivate harmony and mutual understanding both among themselves and with each other . . ."

Lord and Lady Bledisloe with H.R.H. The Duke of Gloucester, at Waitangi 1934.
ALEXANDER TURNBULL LIBRARY

(Above) Mr William Page, honorary architect, explains his distance and direction table on the summit of Mt Bledisloe, 1934.
ALEXANDER TURNBULL LIBRARY

(Right) Tents at Te Tii accommodate visitors at the February 1934 celebrations to mark the Bledisloe Gift.
ALEXANDER TURNBULL LIBRARY

WAITANGI NATIONAL RESERVE

Following the restoration of the Treaty House Waitangi became an emotional focus of New Zealand's constitutional identity. This and the development of the surrounding reserve with recreational facilities, bush plantings and service buildings all helped to draw attention to the area. In 1934 Lord Bledisloe planted the first pohutukawa of many beside the house, thus inaugurating a custom continued by succeeding governors-general and royal visitors.

February 6, 1940 naturally provided a central focus for the nation's centennial celebrations. Construction of the Whare runanga had begun in 1934 shortly after Lord Bledisloe laid the foundation stone. On 6 February 1940 the house was officially opened by the new Governor-General, Lord Galway. Despite the fact that the Whare runanga was situated within the Ngapuhi tribal area it was always intended as a marae for the whole of Aotearoa. Individual carvings represented ancestors of many tribes, all of them carved in the appropriate style under the supervision of master carver Pine Taiapa of Ngati Porou. Pride of place was naturally given to the Ngapuhi ancestor Hineamaru, who delivered her child from beneath her armpit and is represented on a **pou pou** with the head of her child shown in that position. The central pillar or **pou tokomanawa** represents Rahiri, principal ancestor of the Ngati Rahiri of Waitangi. The **pare**, or lintel over the door is carved in what Phillipps calls a vigorous Hauraki style; fourteen pou pou or wall carvings are arranged in pairs and display carvings styles of Waikato, Ngati Maru, Taranaki, Ngatiawa and many others throughout Aotearoa. The great **tekoteko** at the apex of the roofgable represents the ancestor who guided the canoe from Hawaiiki. Particularly unusual are the carved representations of Rangi the Sky Father and Papa the Earth Mother below the **pane,** part of the ridge pole which projects above on the porch.

The 1940 centenary was commemorated by William Page's large stone Hobson Memorial erected behind the Treaty House; it was he who designed the distance and direction table erected on the summit of nearby Mt Bledisloe. In 1958 the sundial on the lawn beside the south side of the house was built to commemorate the visit of Queen Elizabeth II and the Duke of Edinburgh. Finally in 1960 the Busby Memorial Gates at the rear of the house were constructed.

Successive royal visitors and governors-general have planted pohutukawa trees in a grove between the Treaty House and the Whare runanga.

The entry to the Whare runanga features carving from the Hauraki area.

Interior view of the Whare runanga.

William Page's 1940 Hobson Memorial.

Waka party outside the Whare runanga, 6 February 1940.
ALEXANDER TURNBULL LIBRARY

The waka prepares to move offshore, 6 February 1940.
ALEXANDER TURNBULL LIBRARY

The arrival of costumed "European settlers" at the Waitangi celebrations February 1940.
ALEXANDER TURNBULL LIBRARY

The sundial on the south lawn of the Treaty House commemorates the visit of Queen Elizabeth II and the Duke of Edinburgh in 1958.

Lord and Lady Bledisloe beneath the Treaty House's verandah during a return visit to Waitangi in 1947.
ALEXANDER TURNBULL LIBRARY

The distance and direction table at the summit of Mt Bledisloe, highest point of the Waitangi National Reserve.

(Above) Sailors from the Royal New Zealand Navy form a guard of honour at the flagstaff 6 February 1950.
ALEXANDER TURNBULL LIBRARY

(Right) Members of the Royal Tour welcoming party, Waitangi, 28 December 1954. Henare Toka gave the ceremonial challenge.
ALEXANDER TURNBULL LIBRARY

The Queen and the Duke of Edinburgh greet Sir Eruera and Lady Tirikatene in front of the Whare runanga, Waitangi 1963.
ALEXANDER TURNBULL LIBRARY

After 1934 little was done to the Treaty House except essential repairs and maintenance. Not until the 1970s was the necessary additional historical research done into the house's structure. The historian Ruth Ross revealed a great many significant facts about the Busbys' occupation of the former Residency. She recommended to the Trust that because the house's greatest significance lay in its association with the events of 1840, its appearance should reflect the fact. Curiously, the consultant architects decided to furnish the house along lines based upon Miss Agnes Busby's recollections of the house's furnishing at a later date. This had the disturbing effect of confusing the visitor who was now presented with a 1933-restored 1833 house furnished in the style of the 1870s thus giving a spurious impression of Victorian gracious living quite at variance with the lives of James and Agnes Busby in the period of the British Residency. Aidan Challis has pointed out that their "embarrassingly cramped half-house for all its professional design" had no formal dining room or separate parlour—though of course Verge and Busby certainly envisaged both.

The unauthentic, antique-furnished "formal dining room" as it appeared before the 1990 restoration of the Treaty House.
WAITANGI NATIONAL TRUST

The exterior of the original Sydney-designed pre-fabricated portion of the restored Treaty House is painted a slightly darker colour than the later additions, which remain largely unrestored.

The walkway under the skillion allows visitors to inspect the framing of Busby's 1833 Sydney house.

THE 1989-1990 RESTORATION

In 1988 looking ahead to the 1990 sesquicentennial of the signing of the Treaty of Waitangi, the Waitangi National Trust Board commissioned Clive Lucas, O.B.E., an Australian conservation architect and expert in the work of John Verge, to prepare a conservation plan with the aim of resolving these anomalies. Following a thorough analysis of the building fabric and yet further historical research it was proposed by Mr Lucas that the house be fully restored to the Busby family period 1840-1860. There were a number of reasons given for this logical choice. Gummer's 1933 alterations were of great interest in themselves and long familiar to the New Zealand public. Mr Lucas argued that it was possible to present and display the Sydney house effectively within the enlarged structure which now adjoined it .

He divided the project into two stages, the first to involve the complete restoration of the Sydney house and the second, still to be carried out, to attend to the skillion and wings. Work began with the removal of the Tentest interior linings used by Gummer in 1933. The substantially original pre-cut wall and ceiling framing of Australian hardwood was now revealed for the first time since 1933.

As predicted by Mr Lucas, the bottom plate of the original house's back wall had survived intact despite one hundred and fifty six years contact with the ground. The Roman numerals incised on the the framing for ease of assembling prefabricated parts were still clearly visible and Busby's house-in-frame intact.

Now it became possible to display the building's historic fabric to the public while also satisfying its expectation of seeing appropriately furnished rooms. The original framing of the Residency's back wall and the back room were to be permanently visible from within the gutted skillion. Early illustrations of the house justified the retention of the skillion's outer wall; a walkway was built from which the public could now view the original Sydney framing beneath the skillion roof. The original Residency's interiors were restored so as to remove the stately home pretensions which had crept in over previous years.

This involved restoring the mouldings of Australian red cedar doors and then returning them with their architraves to their original positions. Paint applied over the years was stripped by hot air gun and the timber finish brought to life again by applying nugget polish, shellac then wax. Brass door and window furniture was replicated from surviving originals in New South Wales and at Waitangi. French doors on the front elevation which were replaced in kauri in 1933 have now been reconstructed in cedar.

The restored Treaty House's exterior detailing follows the evidence of early photographs. A piece of narrow corner moulding had survived beneath later corner boxing and was replicated for use throughout. The new four-panelled front door replaced the later inauthentic six-panelled one. A new colour scheme based on scrapings taken from frame and upper lights of the front door is in related shades of buff.

The furnishing of the hall, parlour and bedroom have been based on records of acquisitions made by James and Agnes Busby, on surviving family pieces and on illustrations of contemporary colonial interiors in New South Wales and Tasmania. The previous inauthentic collection of furniture has been dispensed with in favour of items known to have been in the Residency before 1840 which have been replicated in detail and correct materials with surfaces distressed to simulate wear and tear on the originals. These include a sofa in Brazilian hardwood and black horsehair and a sideboard in Australian red cedar and kauri—both originals still owned by members of the Busby family. Other so-called "ghost" furniture, including the cot and cradle in the bedroom and the the secretaire in the hall, have been copied from examples of colonial furniture and painted grey to indicate their existence as likely rather than specific forms. Soft furnishings displayed in the Treaty House are true to both contemporary colour and pattern. Thus the restoration of the Sydney house is complete; the next stage proposed for restoration awaits only the will and the finance to complete it.

The four-panelled Australian cedar front door.

The restored dining room reflects the austerity of the British Resident's life at Waitangi between 1833 and 1860.

French casement doors and shutters.

The restored main bedroom.

This simple house has assumed a national significance seemingly out of all proportion to its humble, even confused origins. Not only is it a fine example of colonial Georgian architecture in a splendid location but, more than that, adjacent to the site where the Treaty of Waitangi was signed, it also has a symbolic function which makes its continued restoration and preservation vital.

The Treaty House and its environs have long been a focus for displays of national pride, especially since the passing of the Waitangi Day Act in 1960. They have also witnessed turbulent manifestations of the inevitable tensions as New Zealand in the late twentieth century seeks to define itself as an equitable society which now more than ever before recognises its foundations in what has come to be seen as the partnership guaranteed in the Treaty of Waitangi.

(Below, Left and Right) The Treaty House today.

(Left) A view of the marae at Te Tii looking towards Waitangi photographed in 1880 shortly after the completion of the hall Te Tiriti o Waitangi.
ALEXANDER TURNBULL LIBRARY

(Below) The hall photographed in 1903.
ALEXANDER TURNBULL LIBRARY

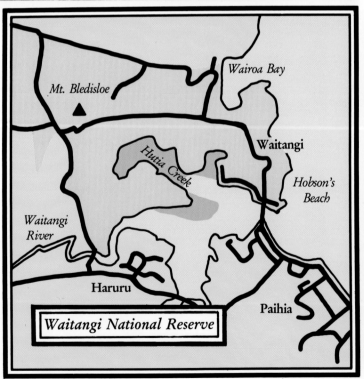

Waitangi National Reserve

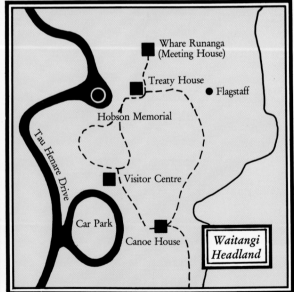

Waitangi Headland

Te Tiriti o Waitangi as it appears today

The canoe shelter

Whare runanga.

The canoe *Ngatokimatawhaorua* which carries eighty warriors is launched annually on 5 February at the ceremonies to commemorate the signing of the Treaty.

Dawn breaks at Te Tii Bay, 6 February 1990, 150th anniversary of the signing of the Treaty of Waitangi.
STEVEN MACLEOD

Waka parties assemble on the beach, 6 February 1990
STEVEN MACLEOD

Protesters make their point at the 1990
celebrations.

(Above Right) Sir Kingi Ihaka, H.M. The Queen,
Governor-General Sir Paul Reeves and the Duke
of Edinburgh at Waitangi February 6 1990.

(Below Right) An impressive moment in the
ceremonies.
PETER SHAW

THE TREATY OF WAITANGI

Her Majesty Victoria Queen of the United Kingdom of Great Britain and Ireland regarding with Her Royal Favor the Native Chiefs and Tribes of New Zealand and anxious to protect their just Rights and Property and to secure to them the enjoyment of Peace and Good Order has deemed it necessary in consequence of the great number of Her Majesty's Subjects who have already settled in New Zealand and the rapid extension of Emigration both from Europe and Australia which is still in progress to constitute and appoint a functionary properly authorized to treat with the Aborigines of New Zealand for the recognition of Her Majesty's sovereign authority over the whole or any part of those islands—Her Majesty therefore being desirous to establish a settled form of Civil Government with a view to avert the evil consequences which must result from the absence of the necessary Laws and Institutions alike to the native population and to Her subjects has been graciously pleased to empower and to authorize me William Hobson a Captain in Her Majesty's Royal Navy Consul and Lieutenant Governor of such parts of New Zealand as may be or hereafter shall be ceded to Her Majesty to invite the confederated and independent Chiefs of New Zealand to concur in the following Articles and Conditions.

Article the first

The Chiefs of the Confederation of the United Tribes of New Zealand and the separate and independent Chiefs who have not become members of the Confederation cede to Her Majesty the Queen of England absolutely and without reservation all the rights and powers of Sovereignty which the said Confederation or Individual Chiefs respectively exercise or possess, or may be supposed to exercise or to possess over their respective Territories as the sole sovereigns thereof.

Article the second

Her Majesty the Queen of England confirms and guarantees to the Chiefs and Tribes of New Zealand and to the respective families and individuals thereof the full exclusive and undisturbed possession of their Lands and Estates Forests Fisheries and other properties which they may collectively or individually possess so long as it is their wish and desire to retain the same in their possession: but the Chiefs of the United Tribes and the individual Chiefs yield to Her Majesty the exclusive right of Preemption over such lands as the proprietors thereof may be disposed to alienate at such prices as may be agreed upon between the respective Proprietors and persons appointed by Her Majesty to treat with them in that behalf.

Article the third

In consideration thereof Her Majesty the Queen of England extends to the Natives of New Zealand Her royal protection and imparts to them all the Rights and Privileges of British Subjects.

[signed] W. Hobson Lieutenant Governor

TE TIRITI O WAITANGI

Ko Wikitoria te Kuini o Ingarani i tana mahara atawai ki nga Rangatira me nga Hapu o Nu Tirani i tana hiahia hoki kia tohungia ki a ratou o ratou rangatiratanga me to ratou wenua, a kia mau tonu hoki te Rongo ki a ratou me te Atanoho hoki kua wakaaro ia he mea tika kia tukua mai tetahi Rangatira—hei kai wakarite ki nga Tangata maori o Nu Tirani—kia wakaaetia e nga Rangatira maori te Kawanatanga o te Kuini ki nga wahikatoa o te wenua nei me nga motu—na te mea hoki he tokomaha ke nga tangata o tona Iwi Kua noho ki tenei wenua, a e haere mai nei.

Na ko te Kuini e hiahia ana kia wakaritea te Kawanatanga kia kaua ai nga kino e puta mai ki te tangata maori ki te Pakeha e noho ture kore ana.

Na kua pai te Kuini kia tukua a hau a Wiremu Hopihona he Kapitana i te Roiara Nawi hei Kawana mo nga wahi katoa o Nu Tirani e tukua aianei amua atu ki te Kuini, e mea atu ana ia ki nga Rangatira o te wakaminenga o nga hapu o Nu Tirani me era Rangatira atu enei ture ka korerotia nei.

Ko te tuatahi

Ko nga Rangatira o te wakaminenga me nga Rangatira katoa hoki ki hai i uru ki taua wakaminenga ka tuku rawa atu ki te Kuini o Ingarani ake tonu atu—te Kawanatanga katoa o o ratou wenua.

Ko te tuarua

Ko te Kuini o Ingarani ka wakarite ka wakaae ki nga Rangatira ki nga hapu —ki nga tangata katoa o Nu Tirani te tino rangatiratanga o o ratou wenua o ratou kainga me o ratou taonga katoa. Otiia ko nga Rangatira o te wakaminenga me nga Rangatira katoa atu ka tuku ki te Kuini te hokonga o era wahi wenua e pai ai te tangata nona te wenua—ki te ritenga o te utu e wakaritea ai e ratou ko te kai hoko e meatia nei e te Kuini hei kai hoko mona.

Ko te tuatoru

Hei wakaritenga mai hoki tenei mo te wakaaetanga ki te Kawanatanga o te Kuini—Ka tiakina e te Kuini o Ingarani nga tangata maori katoa o Nu Tirani ka tukua ki a ratou nga tikanga katoa rite tahi ki ana mea ki nga tangata o Ingarani.

[signed] W. Hobson Consul & Lieutenant Governor

Na ko matou ko nga Rangatira o te Wakamincnga o nga hapu o Nu rirani ka huihui nei ki Waitangi ko matou hoki ko nga Rangatira o Nu Tirani ka kite nei i te ritenga o enei kupu. Ka tangohia ka wakaaetia katoatia e matou, koia ka tohungia ai o matou ingoa o matou tohu.

Ka meatia tenei ki Waitangi i te ono o nga ra o Pepueri i te tau kotahi mano, e waru rau e wa te kau o to tatou Ariki.

This treaty text was signed at Waitangi, 6 February 1840, and thereafter in the north and at Auckland.

INDEX

94

BIBLIOGRAPHY

Binney, Judith. **The Legacy of Guilt: A Life of Thomas Kendall.**
Oxford University Press, Auckland. 1968.

Buick, Lindsay. T. **The Treaty of Waitangi.**
McKay Wellington 1914 (Capper Press 1976)

Challis, Aidan. **A Preliminary Analysis of the Waitangi Treaty House.**
New Zealand Historic Places Trust 1988

Challis, Aidan. **The Restoration of the Treaty House, Waitangi.**
ICOMOS Conference Paper, Russell. 1990.

Darwin, C.R. and Fitzroy, R. **Narrative of the Surveying Voyages of His Majesty's Ships Adventure and Beagle, between the years 1826 and 1836.**
Henry Coburn, London. 1839.

Easdale, Nola. **Missionary and Maori: Kerikeri 1819-1860.**
Te Waihora Press, Lincoln. 1991.

Fill, Barbara. **Report on James Busby, British Resident at Waitangi, 1833-1840.** Waitangi National Trust. 1987.

Frederickson, Clayton. **A Preliminary Historical and Archeological Survey of the Waitangi National Reserve.**
Department of Conservation Science and Research Internal Report No.25.

McLean, Martin. **The Garden of New Zealand. A History of the Waitangi Treaty House and Grounds from Pre-European Times to the Present.**
Department of Conservation Science and Research Internal Report No.76.

Lee, Jack. **I Have Named it Bay of Islands.**
Hodder and Stoughton, Auckland. 1987.

Lucas, Clive, Stapleton and Partners Pty Ltd. **The Treaty House, Waitangi, Bay of Islands, New Zealand.**
Conservation Analysis and Draft Conservation Policy. Sydney. 1989.

McCoomb, Ralph. **Report on the Restoration of the Treaty House, Waitangi, Bay of Islands, 1933.** (unpublished)

Minson, Marian. **Encounter with Eden. New Zealand 1770-1870.**
Paintings and Drawings from the Rex Nan Kivell Collection, National Library of Australia.
Alexander Turnbull Library/Te Puna Matauranga o Aotearoa, Wellington. 1990.

Ollivier, Isabel. **Early Eyewitness Accounts of Maori Life: 2.**
(transcribed and translated). Extracts from Journals relating to the visit to New Zealand in May-July 1772 of the French ships Mascarin and Marquis de Castries under the command of M-J. Marion du Fresne.
Alexander Turnbull Library Endowment Trust with Indosuez New Zealand Limited, Wellington. 1985.

Orange, Claudia. **The Treaty of Waitangi,**
Allen and Unwin, Wellington. 1987

Orange, Claudia. **An Illustrated History of the Treaty of Waitangi.**
Allen and Unwin, Wellington. 1990.

Phillipps, W.J. **Carved Maori Houses of the Western and Northern Areas of New Zealand.**
Dominion Museum/Government Printer, Wellington 1955.

Ramsden, Eric. **Busby of Waitangi: H.M.'s Resident in New Zealand, 1833-40.**
Reed, Wellington. 1942.

Reed, Vernon. **The Gift of Waitangi: A History of the Bledisloe Gift.**
Reed, Wellington. 1957.

Ross, Ruth. **Research Report on the old British Residency at Waitangi.**
Waitangi National Trust. 1975

Salmond, Anne. **Two Worlds: First Meetings Between Maori and Europeans 1642-1772**
Viking, Auckland 1991

Simpson, Miria. **Nga Tohu o Te Tiriti. Making a mark. The Signatories to the Treaty of Waitangi.**
National Library of New Zealand, Wellington. 1990.

Sinclair, Keith (ed.) **The Oxford History of New Zealand**.
Oxford University Press, Auckland. 1990.

Sissons, J. Wi Hongi, W. and Hohepa, P. **The Puriri trees are
Laughing: A Political history of Ngapuhi in the Inland Bay of
Islands**. Polynesian Society Memoir 46. 1987.

The Dictionary of New Zealand Biography. Vol.1. 1769-1869.
Allen and Unwin Limited and Department of Internal Affairs. 1990.

GLOSSARY OF MAORI TERMS

whare—house
tangata whenua—people of the land
hapu—sub-section of a tribe
karakia—incantation
taniwha—water demon
Ngati—tribal prefix
utu—revenge
Pakeha—person of European descent
atua—ancestral spirit, god
pa—fortified village
taua muru—plundering party
tangi—funeral
hahunga—the bone lifting ceremony which takes place before
        re-burial
wahi tapu—sacred place

moko—facial tattoo
hongi—traditional Maori greeting involving the pressing of noses
        together
mere—short flat stone weapon
kawanatanga—government
pou pou—upright supports of the wall frame of a building
pou tokomanawa—carved central post inside a meeting house
pare—carved timber piece over the door of a whare
tekoteko—carved figure at the gable of a house
pane—head
whare runanga—council house
marae—the enclosed space in front of a meeting house
tapu—sacred
waka—canoe
waka taua—war canoe

NOTE: These words are printed in bold type in the text of the book where
they first occur and are listed above in the same order.